THE SWEETNESS OF HONEY
AND THE STING OF BEES

1

NOTHING IS SWEETER THAN LOVE;
ALL OTHER BLISS COMES SECOND.
AND COMPARED TO IT,
EVEN HONEY IS TOO BITTER
TO HOLD IN MY MOUTH.

NOSSIS
The Greek Anthology V.170

THE SWEETNESS OF HONEY AND THE STING OF BEES
© Michelle Lovric 1997
Conceived and compiled by Michelle Lovric, Covent Garden, London
Translations by Michelle Lovric and Nikiforos Doxiadis Mardas
Translations © Michelle Lovric 1997
Designed by Michelle Lovric and Lisa Pentreath
Distressed backgrounds photographed by Debbie Patterson
Technical editor: Carol Franklin. Feline design assistants: Tuck and Spin

Published in 1997 and distributed by
Stewart, Tabori & Chang,
a division of U.S. Media Holdings, Inc.
115 West 18th Street, New York, N Y 10011

Distributed in Canada by
General Publishing Company Ltd.
30 Lesmill Road
Don Mills, Ontario, M3B 2T6, Canada

Distributed in Australia by
Peribo Pty Ltd.
58 Beaumont Road
Mount Kuring-gai, NSW 2080, Australia

Distributed in all other territories by
Grantham Book Services Ltd.
Isaac Newton Way, Alma Park Industrial Estate
Grantham, Lincolnshire, NG31 9SD, England

Library of Congress Catalog Card Number:
96-66509

ISBN 1-55670-680-4

Repro by Ripe Reprographics Ltd., England
Printed in China by Imago

10 9 8 7 6 5 4 3 2 1

NOTE:

Most of the Fayum portraits in this book were originally published in THE MYSTERIOUS FAYUM
PORTRAITS, Faces from Ancient Egypt, by Euphrosyne Doxiadis, available from Harry N. Abrams Inc.,
New York, ISBN 0-8109-3331-4 originally published in 1995 by Thames and Hudson Ltd., London.

ACKNOWLEDGEMENTS

The editors gratefully acknowledge the permission of the following to reproduce copyrighted
material in this book. Every effort has been made to locate copyright-holders. In the event that
we have unwillingly or inadvertently admitted the proper notification, the editors would be
grateful to hear from the copyright-holder and amend any subsequent editions accordingly.

TEXTUAL

Love Lyrics of Ancient Egypt, translated by Barbara Hughes Fowler. © 1994 by the
University of North Carolina Press. Used by permission of the publisher.
Translation of fragment 31 by Sappho on page 61 by William Carlos Williams from
Paterson, Book Five, published by Carcanet Press Limited and New Directions Publishing
Corporation. © 1958 William Carlos Williams.

ILLUSTRATIVE

Illustrations from Heck's Pictorial Archive of Art and Architecture edited by J.G. Heck,
published by Dover Publications Inc. © 1994 Dover Publications Inc.

Images on pages 1, 17, 55, 68, 80 courtesy of the Bildarchiv Preussischer Kulturbesitz,
Staatlich Museen zu Berlin, photographed by I. Geske.

Images on pages 7(r), 30, 48, 86 courtesy of the Archäologisches Institut und Akademisches
Kunstmuseum der Universität Bonn, photographed by Wolfgang Klein.

Images on the front cover and pages 4, 16, 34, 72, 96 from the Louvre, Paris
courtesy of Réunion des Musées Nationaux, photographed by Gérard Blot.

Images on pages 3(r), 6(r), 7(m), 16, 23, 33, 51, 56, 74/5, 91(t) courtesy of the Pushkin Museum,
Moscow, photographed by L. Gavrilova.

Images on front jacket flap and pages 3(l), 6(l/m), 7(l), 8, 20, 21, 22(l), 24, 25, 29, 36, 39, 41,
42, 47, 49, 53, 56, 59, 60/1, 66, 70, 76, 81, 82/3, 85, 87, 89, 90, 91(l&b), 94/5 courtesy of the
Egyptian Museum, Cairo, and Euphrosyne Doxiadis, photographed by Lucinda Douglas-Menzies.

Images on pages 9, 12, 15, 19, 43, 45, 50, 65, 79, 88, 92 from the British Museum,
London, courtesy of the Trustees of the British Museum.

Images on reverse of endpapers, 22(l), 27, 28, 37, 69, 84, 91(r) courtesy of
The Manchester Museum, The University of Manchester.

Images on the back cover and pages 41, 62/3, 77 courtesy of Nefer Collection, Switzerland.

Images on pages 38, 58 courtesy of a private collection.

THIS BOOK IS DEDICATED TO SUZANNE WOLSTENHOLME,
"a gift to death from love"

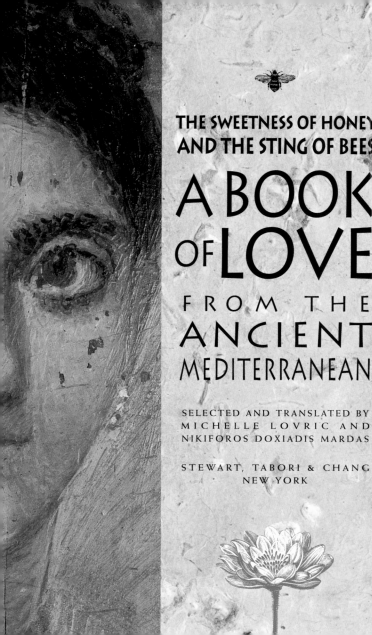

THE SWEETNESS OF HONEY
AND THE STING OF BEES

A BOOK
OF LOVE

FROM THE
ANCIENT
MEDITERRANEAN

SELECTED AND TRANSLATED BY
MICHELLE LOVRIC AND
NIKIFOROS DOXIADIS MARDAS

STEWART, TABORI & CHANG
NEW YORK

CONTENTS

PAGE 6   **ENDURING IMAGES OF LOVE AND PASSION**
– notes on the text and provenance of this book

PAGE 10   **GODS AND POETS**

PAGE 12   *The blood around men's hearts is their thinking*
SWEET HONEYED MYSTERY OF LOVE

PAGE 16   *Love, you distil desire upon the eyes*
THE BEAUTIFUL LOVED ONE

PAGE 30   *I send you sweet perfume*
GIFTS OF LOVE

PAGE 32   *Your mouth is a hook with madness in its barb*
SEDUCTION

PAGE 45   *Love the limb-loosener sweeps me away*
SENSUALITY

PAGE 52   *Love convulsed my heart*
ADDICTED TO LOVE

PAGE 62   *Your love is mixed in my limbs*
ONE SOUL IN TWO BODIES

PAGE 65   *Safe and sacrosant*
THE PROTECTIVE ARMS OF LOVE

PAGE 68   *The sweetness of honey and the sting of bees*
PLEASURE AND PAIN

PAGE 82   *Her heart is devoured by pain*
ABSENCE AND LONGING

PAGE 87   *I know your promises are empty*
BETRAYAL

PAGE 93   *The cold imprint of my remembered kisses*
REGRETS

PAGE 94   *I will sit bound by the altars of inviolable Venus*
UNDYING LOVE

5

ENDURING IMAGES

NOTES ON THE TEXT AND PROVENANCE OF THIS BOOK

THIS BOOK IS FOR THE MELTING VIRGIN
RESPONDING TO HER BELOVED,
AND FOR THE UNSOPHISTICATED BOY
TOUCHED BY NEW AND UNKNOWN TENDERNESS.
SO THAT EVERY YOUNG PERSON,
IMPALED, AS I AM, ON THE ARROW OF LOVE,
SHALL RECOGNIZE HERE THE SYMPTOMS OF THEIR OWN FEVER,
AND ASK, IN UTTER ASTONISHMENT:
"HOW COULD THIS POET KNOW THE STORY OF MY LIFE?
AND WRITE THIS BOOK
– THE MIRROR OF MY OWN MELODRAMA? "

OVID
Amores II. 1

VI

OF LOVE & PASSION

UNLIKE WAR OR EMPIRE, LOVE LEAVES LITTLE TRACE FOR THE ARCHAEOLOGISTS: ONLY THE WRITTEN KISSES SURVIVE THE BRIEF INCANDESCENT ALCHEMY OF HUMAN PASSION. EZRA POUND ONCE DESCRIBED TRANSLATIONS OF ARCHAIC AUTHORS AS "BLOOD BROUGHT TO GHOSTS". THIS BOOK IS INTENDED TO BREATHE WARM LIFE INTO THE LOVE POEMS AND LETTERS OF BOTH THE GREAT AND UNKNOWN VANISHED LOVERS OF THE ANCIENT MEDITERRANEAN. FOR MANY, THE GREAT SURPRISE WILL BE TO DISCOVER THAT THEIR THOUSAND-YEAR-OLD WORDS ARE AS FRESH, PASSIONATE AND SOMETIMES AS IRREVERANT AS TODAY'S RAW SONG LYRICS: PLAYING, FIGHTING, FLIRTING, THE WRITINGS OF THE ANCIENT POETS ARE NOT A SHADOW BUT A MIRROR OF OUR OWN EXPERIENCES.

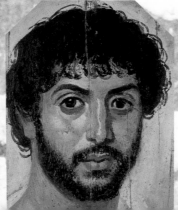

To illustrate these paradoxically contemporary poems, I needed antique images of staggering modernity — and I was fortunate enough to find them.

When I made the first of four trips to Egypt early in the 1990s, it was not the pyramids or the temples which remained in my mind: it was a room in Cairo's archaeological museum which haunted me — a room full of powerful personalities, all asserting themselves eloquently, eerily alive in that place full of silent statuary. These people have become known as the Fayum portraits, the painted faces from mummy cases, discovered in the Greek cemeteries of Roman Egypt during the past 100 years.

The portraits are the most intense and fascinating personal art to survive the ancient world. The faces are not invariably beautiful, but they are all profoundly rich in expression. They seem about to speak. To me, these vibrant faces express all the sweet wonderment, honeyed seductions and unmendable pains of love, with only a gorgeous patina of the past to betray their antiquity. Painted in encaustic or tempera, which has preserved their colours, they lend veracity to the Egyptian belief that every soul had its double-image, which would fly from the tomb and live for ever. And now, happily, many more people will have a chance to encounter these unforgettable faces — at exhibitions

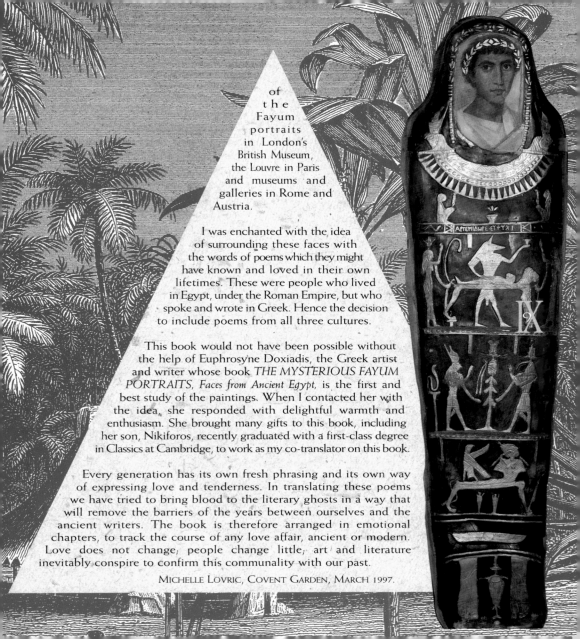

of
t h e
Fayum
portraits
in London's
British Museum,
the Louvre in Paris
and museums and
galleries in Rome and
Austria.

I was enchanted with the idea
of surrounding these faces with
the words of poems which they might
have known and loved in their own
lifetimes. These were people who lived
in Egypt, under the Roman Empire, but who
spoke and wrote in Greek. Hence the decision
to include poems from all three cultures.

This book would not have been possible without
the help of Euphrosyne Doxiadis, the Greek artist
and writer whose book *THE MYSTERIOUS FAYUM
PORTRAITS, Faces from Ancient Egypt*, is the first and
best study of the paintings. When I contacted her with
the idea, she responded with delightful warmth and
enthusiasm. She brought many gifts to this book, including
her son, Nikiforos, recently graduated with a first-class degree
in Classics at Cambridge, to work as my co-translator on this book.

Every generation has its own fresh phrasing and its own way
of expressing love and tenderness. In translating these poems
we have tried to bring blood to the literary ghosts in a way that
will remove the barriers of the years between ourselves and the
ancient writers. The book is therefore arranged in emotional
chapters, to track the course of any love affair, ancient or modern.
Love does not change; people change little; art and literature
inevitably conspire to confirm this communality with our past.

MICHELLE LOVRIC, COVENT GARDEN, MARCH 1997.

GODS

10

GODS

(THE GREEK NAMES ARE ALWAYS FIRST)

APHRODITE / VENUS
Goddess of Love, Beauty and
Fertility. She was also known as
Kypris, and the **Kyprian**, because
of her important sanctuary at
Paphos on the island of Cyprus,
and as the **Kytherean**, because
she was supposed to have been
born on the sea-foam near the
Greek island of Kythera.

ARTEMIS / DIANA
Goddess of Wildlife, usually
represented as a virgin huntress,
though her worship was also
associated with Child-birth.

ATHENA / MINERVA
A virgin War Goddess, usually
portrayed as armed for battle.
She was the patron Goddess of
Athens, and was closely associated
with Skill, Art and Wisdom.

DIONYSOS (BAKCHOS)
LIBER (BACCHUS)
God of Wine and Ecstasy, usually
represented as reclining with
grapes or a wine-cup.

EROS / CUPID.
God of Love. In early Greek
literature he was the beautiful
but cruel personification of
physical desire. The familiar
image of him as the mischievous
little son of **Aphrodite / Venus**,
was a later literary conception
which emerged over time and
which was well-developed by
the Hellenistic era. For just such
a portrait see Meleager's poem
on page 76.

POETS

Adaios (fl. 1st century BC)
of Macedon.

Agathias Scholasticus (c. 536–82)
practised law in Constantinople
and was married to the daughter
of the poet Paulos whose work
also appears in this book.

Alkaios (fl. 200 BC) of Messene.
Not to be confused with the
famous 7th century BC lyric
poet from Lesbos.

Alkman (fl. second half of the
7th century BC) of Sparta. It is
said that pro-Athenian sources
named him a Lydian to avoid
attributing any culture to their
enemies.

Anakreon (c. 570–485 BC) of
Teos in Asia Minor. Famous for
his lyrical celebrations of the
twinned joys of love and wine.

The Anakreontea. A collection
of poems composed over several
centuries by writers whose work
reflects the influence of Anakreon
in both style and content.

Antiphilos (fl. 1st century)
of Byzantium.

Apollonius Rhodius
(c. 295– 215 BC) Hellenistic
poet from Alexandria.

Asklepiades (fl. c. 290 BC) of
Samos. He is attributed with
introducing the symbols of
Love the archer, and the baby
Eros into the love epigram.

Bianor (fl. 1st century) of
Bithynia.

Bion (fl. c. 100 BC) of Phlossa in
Asia Minor.

Catullus (Gaius Valerius
Catullus) (c. 84–54 BC) Roman
poet born in Verona. His most
famous love poems concern his
stormy affair with "Lesbia",
almost certainly the notorious
Clodia, wife of Quintus
Metellus Celer.

Dioskorides (fl. 230 BC) of
Nikopolis.

Empedokles (c. 493–433 BC)
of Akragas in Sicily. Greek
philosopher, scientist, poet,
statesman, and, reputedly,
mystic and miracle-worker.

Euenos (fl. 1st century)
Greek poet.

Euripides (c. 484–406 BC)
Greek dramatist, and youngest
of the three great Athenian
tragedians.

The Garland of Sulpicia. Five
poems on the love of the poetess
Sulpicia for Cerinthus which
are grouped with the work of,
and were conceivably composed
by the Roman poet Tibullus.

Gauradas (dates unknown)
Greek poet.

The Greek Anthology.
An amalgamation of earlier
collections, the Anthology of
over 4000 epigrams preserves

THESE BEINGS, MYTHICAL AND LITERARY

& Poets

an enormous range of ancient poetry from across several centuries, some of it of exceptional quality. Books 5 and 12 are collections of love poetry.

Hesiod (fl. c. 700 BC) one of the earliest known Greek poets.

Hippokrates (c. 460–377 BC) of Kos. Greek physician.

Homer (fl. 8th century BC) of Chios or Samos. Greek epic poet in the oral tradition, author of *The Iliad* and *The Odyssey*.

Homeric Hymns. The 33 Hymns were written in Greek some time between the 8th and the 6th centuries BC. They are sometimes, but controversially, attributed to the author of *The Iliad* and *The Odyssey*.

Horace (Quintus Horatius Flaccus) (65–8 BC) Roman poet.

Ibykos (fl. mid 6th century BC) of Rhegium in southern Italy. Greek lyric poet.

Kallimachos (c. 305–240 BC) of Kyrene. Hellenistic poet who lived in Alexandria, and whose prolific work had a strong influence on such Roman poets as Catullus, Ovid and Propertius.

Longus (probably mid 3rd century) Greek writer, creator of the pastoral romance.

Lucretius (Titus Lucretius Carus) (94–55 BC) Roman philosopher and poet.

Lygdamus (fl. late 1st century BC) Roman love elegist.

Martial (Marcus Valerius Martialis) (c. 40–103) Roman poet, born at Bilbilis in Spain.

Macedonius (fl. mid 6th century) held the by now honorary post of Consul under the Emperor Justinian at Constantinople.

Marcus Argentarius (fl. early 1st century) Greek poet.

Meleager (fl. 100 BC) of Gadara in Syria. Greek poet and philosopher.

Nossis (fl. c. 300 BC) of Locri in southern Italy. Greek poetess.

Ovid (Publius Ovidius Naso) (c. 43 BC–18 AD) Roman poet whose brilliantly inventive, and often subversive, poetry won him great fame but led to his banishment to the Black Sea by the Emperor Augustus.

Paulos Silentiarius (fl. mid 6th century) courtier of the Emperor Justinian at Constantinople.

Petronius (Titus Petronius Arbiter) (fl. 1st century) Roman writer, author of *The Satyricon*, and possibly the courtier by that name of the Emperor Nero.

Philodemos (c. 110–30 BC) of Gadara.

Pindar (518–438 BC) of Kynoskephalae near Thebes. Greek lyric poet.

Plato (427–347 BC) Athenian philosopher.

Polemon (fl. 1st century BC) Ruler of Pontus.

Propertius (Sextus Propertius) (c. 50–15 BC) Roman poet whose love elegies were mostly dedicated to "Cynthia", probably a Greek pseudonym for his real-life mistress, Hostia.

Pseudo-Lucian. Attribution given to a series of humorous dialogues written in Greek in the style of the writer Lucian (c. 115–180).

Rufinus (dates uncertain, 2nd–5th century) Greek poet probably from Asia Minor.

Rufinus Domesticus (dates unknown) Greek poet.

Sappho (fl. c. 600 BC) of Eresos on the island of Lesbos. Greek lyric poetess.

Sophokles (c. 496–406 BC) Greek dramatist, one of the three great Athenian tragedians.

Theokritos (early 3rd century BC) of Syracuse in Sicily. Greek bucolic poet.

Tibullus (Albius Tibullus) (c. 55–19 BC) Roman love elegist.

Virgil (Publius Vergilius Maro) (70–19 BC) Roman poet, author of the Augustan epic *The Aeneid*.

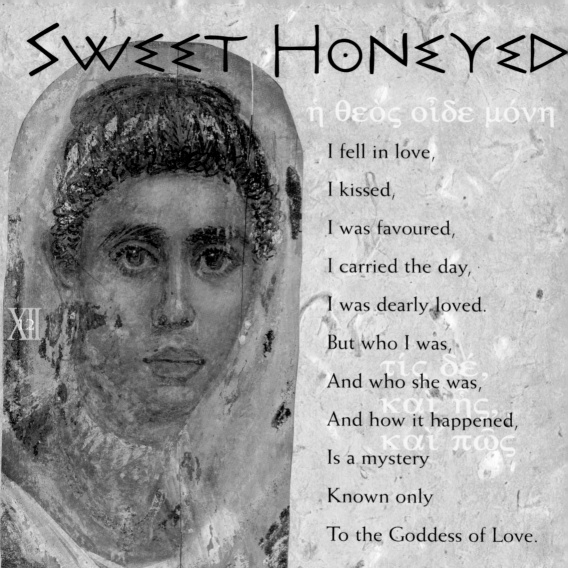

SWEET HONEYED

ἡ θεὸς οἶδε μόνη

I fell in love,

I kissed,

I was favoured,

I carried the day,

I was dearly loved.

But who I was,

And who she was,

And how it happened,

Is a mystery

Known only

To the Goddess of Love.

UNKNOWN GREEK POET
The Greek Anthology V.51

MYSTERY OF LOVE

ἄδιον οὐδὲν ἔρωτος

NOTHING IS SWEETER THAN LOVE;
ALL OTHER BLISS COMES SECOND.
AND COMPARED TO IT,
EVEN HONEY IS TOO BITTER
TO HOLD IN MY MOUTH.

NOSSIS
The Greek Anthology V.170

Once, when I was weaving a garland,

I found Love among the roses.

I grabbed him up by the wings,

I dropped him into my wine cup,

Picked it up, and drank him down.

And now, inside my body,

He tickles me deliciously with his wings.

THE ANAKREONTEA
poem 6

XII

13

KISSING ANTIOCHOS, THE MOST BEAUTIFUL OF YOUTHS,
I TASTED THE DELICIOUS HONEY OF THE SOUL.

MELEAGER
The Greek Anthology XII.133

All things are susceptible to Love:
Fire, water and the snows of Scythia.

LONGUS
Daphnis and Chloe III

14

HOW COULD WE LIVE WITHOUT THE ROSE?
ROSE-FINGERED DAWN, ROSY-ARMED NYMPHS,
ROSE-COMPLEXIONED APHRODITE

THE ANAKREONTEA
poem 55

Wild Love,
IS THERE ANYTHING YOU CANNOT FORCE UPON THE HUMAN HEART?

VIRGIL
Aeneid IV (Dido and Aeneas)

"Goddess of Love, you hold sway over
The unbending hearts of Gods and mortals,
And with you soars Eros, enfolding them all
In his swift and dappled wings.
He flies over the earth
And over the melodious brine-filled sea.
And he spreads his enchantment,
Setting fires in maddened hearts
With his flickering golden wing..."

EURIPIDES
Hippolytos
From an ode sung by the chorus on the play's central theme:
the deadly dangers of ignoring the power of Aphrodite

15

THE BLOOD AROUND MEN'S HEARTS
is their thinking.

EMPEDOKLES *fragment 105*

The Beautiful Loved One

LOVE, CONSTRUCTED AS A LADDER OF PLEASURE, HAS, AS ITS FIRST STEP, **SIGHT.**

NO ONE EVER HAS,
AND NO ONE EVER WILL,
ESCAPE LOVE,
NOT WHILE THERE IS BEAUTY,
AND NOT WHILE EYES CAN SEE.

LONGUS
Daphnis and Chloe I

PSEUDO-LUCIAN
Erotes

16

The dear face of Nicarete,
Which often appeared at the high windows,
Was one day seared by desire.
Bright lightning flashed
From the sweet gaze of Kleophon,
As he stood on the doorstep,
And struck her down.

ASKLEPIADES
The Greek Anthology V.153

MY
IMAGE
IS
STAMPED
ON
YOUR
MOLTEN
HEART...
YOUR
BEAUTY
IS
ENGRAVED
ON
MY
SQUL.

PAULOS SILENTIARIUS
The Greek Anthology V.274

SOME SAY THAT THE MOST BEAUTIFUL THING ON THIS DARK EARTH

IS A HOST OF HORSEMEN, OTHERS THAT IT IS AN ARMY OF FOOT-SOLDIERS,

ἰππήων

πεσδῶν

AND OTHERS THAT IT IS A FLEET OF SHIPS; BUT I SAY IT IS WHAT YOU LOVE.

νάων

SAPPHO
fragment 16

18 "I come to you on bended knee, Queen. *Are you god or mortal?*
If you are one of the immortals who hold sway over the immense Heavens,
I think that in beauty, stature and nature,
You are most like Artemis, daughter of mighty Zeus.
But if you are one of the mortals who live on the earth,
Three-times-blessed are your father and your revered mother,
Three-times-blessed are your brothers and sisters.
Their hearts must always warm with happiness,
When they watch you, their rosebud just opening, enter the dance.
But blessed beyond all others is the man who courts you
With nuptial gifts and leads you to his home.
Never have I set my eyes upon such beauty, in either man or woman.
I look at you and I am bedazzled..."

HOMER
Odyssey VI
From the speech of Odysseus, delivered dressed only in an improvised loin-cloth, to the beautiful Nausicaa, daughter of King Alcinous. He has just swum ashore to their island kingdom of Scheria from his wrecked boat.

allure

THE RIVER IS LIKE WINE,

its reeds the god Ptah,

SEKHMET ITS LOTUS BUDS,

Yadit its lotus buds, 19

NEFERTEM ITS LOTUS BUDS,

the earth has grown light,

THROUGH MY SISTER'S LOVELINESS.

HARRIS PAPYRUS, 19TH DYNASTY,
NEW KINGDOM EGYPT.
Translated by Barbara Hughes Fowler, 1994.
Ptah was the god of Truth and Judgement after Death,
Sekhmet the lioness-god of War. Nefertem was the son of Sekhmet and
Ptah. Yadit is probably a minor goddess.

Lesbia is beautiful, not only the loveliest of all,
But she's the one who's stolen all the allure
From all the rest.

CATULLUS *poem 86*

τὰν ἐπ' ὄσσοισ' ὀμπέτασον χάριν

UNFURL THE

NATURE GAVE
HORNS TO BULLS
HOOVES TO HORSES
SPEED TO HARES
A GAPING MAW OF TEETH
TO THE LIONS
SWIMMING TO FISH,
FLIGHT TO BIRDS,
WISDOM TO MEN,
BUT FOR WOMEN,
SHE HAD NOTHING LEFT.
So what then?
SHE GAVE THEM
BEAUTY,
THE EQUAL OF ANY
SHIELD,
THE EQUAL OF ANY SPEAR.
EVEN STRONGER
THAN STEEL
OR FIRE
IS A BEAUTIFUL WOMAN.

THE ANAKREONTEA
poem 24

LOVELINESS IN YOUR EYES

SAPPHO
fragment 138

The Muses tied up Eros
With garlands,
And handed him over to Beauty.
And now the Kytherean
Brings ransom,
Seeking to have Eros released.
But even if he was set free
He would not leave. He would stay,
For he has already learnt
To be Beauty's slave.

THE ANAKREONTEA
poem 19

THEY DRIVE ME WILD, THOSE FLUENT ROSE-RED LIPS,
GATEWAYS TO HER NECTAR-FLAVOURED MOUTH,
   THEY DISSOLVE MY SOUL.
HER PUPILS, ELECTRIFYING UNDER HER DARK BROWS,
SET NETS AND TRAPS FOR MY HEART.
AND HER SOFT BREASTS GLOSSY AS POURED CREAM,
NESTLE TOGETHER SWEETLY, VOLUPTUOUSLY AND DELECTABLY
MORE PERFECT THAN THE PETALS OF ANY ROSEBUD.

DIOSKORIDES
The Greek Anthology V.56

THE GAZE OF THE

XXII

With limb-loosening desire ...
She gazes at me, more meltingly
than Sleep or DEATH.

ALKMAN
fragment 3

CYNTHIA FIRST
ENSNARED ME
WITH HER EYES –
ME, A WRETCH
NEVER BEFORE
TOUCHED BY
DESIRE.

PROPERTIUS
Elegies I.1

It was not the cavalry,
Or the infantry,
Or even the navy,
But another strange kind of army
That destroyed me,
Striking me down with her **eyes.**

THE ANAKREONTEA
poem 26

LOVER

I know only one utterly beautiful thing,
My ravenous eye knows only one thing:
That is to look at Mysikos.
To everything else, I am blind.

MELEAGER
The Greek Anthology XII. 106

Her necklace is made of buds.

Her bones are delicate reeds.

She wears a signet ring

and has a lotus in

her hand. I kiss her

before everyone that

they all may see my love.

She enraptures my heart, and when

she sees me, I am refreshed.

20TH DYNASTY, NEW KINGDOM EGYPT.
Translated by Barbara Hughes Fowler, 1994.

23

YOUR KISS IS LACED WITH BIRDLIME,
AND YOUR EYES, TIMARION, WITH FIRE.
LOOK AT ME, AND I BURN,
TOUCH ME AND I AM CAUGHT.

MELEAGER
The Greek Anthology V. 96

I love KLEOBOULOS, I am mad about KLEOBOULOS, I gaze at KLEOBOULOS.

ANAKREON fragment 359

EYES

XXIV

HER EYES ARE GOLDEN STAR-FIRE,
HER CHEEKS OF CRYSTAL,
HER MOUTH ROSIER
THAN A WINE-RED
FLOWER BUD.
HER NECK IS CARVED
FROM SNOWY MARBLE,
HER BREASTS
ARE SOFTLY LUMINOUS,
HER FEET MORE SILVERY
THAN THOSE OF
THE WATER-NYMPH
THETIS.

RUFINUS
The Greek Anthology V.48
Thetis, destined to bear a son greater than
his father, was the mother of the Greek hero
Achilles.

LOVE, YOU DISTIL

AND STARS

You're star-gazing, my star?
I wish that I could be the Sky,
With all those eyes to look at you.

PLATO
The Greek Anthology VII.669

YOUR BODY IS ALL GRACE
YOUR EYES ... HONEY,
THE LOVE FLOWS INTO
YOUR LONGED-FOR FACE.

SAPPHO
fragment 112

EURIPIDES
Hippolytos

ƆƐSIRƐ UPON MY ƐYƐS

The Art of Love

WHO SCULPTED THE SEA?
What wild art poured the waves on to a silver salver?
Who carved soft white Kypris on the back of the sea,
His soul soaring to the gods?
He showed her naked, hiding with the sea-foam
Only that which must remain hidden.

THE ANAKREONTEA
poem 57

26

Come, best of painters,

Paint, best of painters,
Master of the Rhodian art,
Paint my absent lover
Exactly as I describe her.
Paint for me, please, her hair,
Soft and dark.
Paint it, if the wax is willing,
So that it exhales sweetness.
Paint her whole cheek,
And in the shade of her flowing dark hair
Paint her ivory forehead.
Her eyebrows should not meet,
Nor, please, should they be wide apart,
But let the dark rims of her eyelids
Almost join in an imperceptible frown,
As they do in life.
Now make her gaze of fire,
As it really is,
With eyes bright like Athena's
And moist like the Kytherean's.
Paint her cheeks and nose
With rose petals swimming in milk,
And paint her lips like Peitho's,
Irresistibly kissable.
Under her soft chin,
Let all the Graces dance
Around her marble neck.
Dress her in robes of light purple,
But make it transparent in places,
To reveal through glimpses of flesh,
The true beauty of her body.
Now stand back — I can see her.
Portrait, I think you're about to speak!

THE ANAKREONTEA
*poem 16. The "Rhodian art" is painting and Peitho
is the personification of persuasiveness.*

XXVII
27

τὸ δὲ βλέμμα νῦν ἀληθῶς ἀπὸ τοῦ πυρὸς ποίησον

true love

What is beautiful lasts only as long as it is looked upon,
But what is good will soon also be beautiful.

σελίνων SAPPHO ουλοτέρη
fragment 50

PHILAENION IS SHORT AND SOMEWHAT SWARTHY
BUT HER HAIR IS CURLIER THAN PARSLEY,
HER SKIN IS SOFTER THAN DUCKLING'S DOWN,
AND HER VOICE SWAYS WITH MORE MAGIC
THAN THE GIRDLE OF APHRODITE.
SHE GIVES ME EVERYTHING,
AND ALMOST NEVER ASKS FOR ANYTHING IN RETURN.
SO, LET PHILAENION BE MY ONE AND ONLY,
GOLDEN KYPRIS,
At least until I find an even better one.

PHILODEMUS
The Greek Anthology V.121

is blind

A swarthy one is "honey-coloured",
A foul and filthy one is "au naturelle"...
A stringy and wooden one is "a gazelle",
A squat dwarf is "one of the Graces" and "full of wit",
A monstrous huge one is "phenomenal" and "full of grandeur",
If she stammers and can't speak, "she has a charming lisp",
A mute one is "shy",
A shameless, hateful chatterbox is "a little cracker",
One who looks starved to the point of death is "a slender sweetheart"...
One with fat lips is "all kiss".

LUCRETIUS
De Rerum Natura IV

TO ME YOU ARE PRETTY ENOUGH,
As long as you come to me often enough.

PROPERTIUS
Elegies II.18

GIFTS of LOVE

CHUC ADES, O FORMOSE PUER

Come to me, beautiful boy:
see how the nymphs bring you
lilies in heaped baskets, how for
you the fair water-nymph, plucking
pale violets and the heads of poppies,
mixes narcissus and sweet-smelling
fennel-flower; then, entwining them
30 with cassia and other delicious
herbs, she embroiders the delicate
hyacinth with the golden marigold.
I myself will gather quinces pale
with down, and chestnuts, which
   my Amaryllis
      LOVED

VIRGIL
Eclogue 2

**DO NOT LET A FEMALE IN A TEMPTING DRESS GET THE BETTER OF
YOU WITH HER WHEEDLING WAYS AND HER SMOOTH TONGUE:**
she is after your granary.

HESIOD *Works and Days*

I SEND YOU *sweet perfume,* **BUT THE COMPLIMENT IS TO THE** *perfume,* **NOT TO YOU. FOR YOU ARE ABLE TO** *perfume* **EVEN THE** *perfume.*

UNKNOWN GREEK POET
The Greek Anthology V.91

"Ερωs

LOVE
IS
A
NAKED
CHILD...
HE
HAS
NO
POCKET
TO
HOLD
MONEY
IN.

OVID
Amores I.10

31

I am last harvest's quince, still fresh,
Preserved in a young skin,
Unblemished, unwrinkled, downy as a new-born,
Not yet parted from my leafy stem,
A rare prize from the kingdom of Winter.
But for you, Queen of my heart,
Even the snows and frosts can bear fruit like this.

ANTIPHILOS
The Greek Anthology VI.252

SEDUCTION

It's happening again.
Pitching a purple ball at me,
Golden-haired Love musters me
To play with the girl
With the kaleidoscopic sandals.

ANAKREON
fragment 358   νήνι ποικιλοσαμβάλῳ

32

THE WILL-POWER OF THE LOVER IS STORMED BY INNUMERABLE ARTS,
JUST AS A ROCK IN THE SEA IS BEATEN BY THE WAVES FROM EVERY SIDE.

OVID
Remedia Amoris

Love is born naked, and does not love beauty embellished by artifice.
    See what colours the earth brings forth untilled,
And how much more vigorously ivy prospers in the wild,
    And how much lovelier is the Arbutus tree when it springs up in lonely groves,
And how unschooled water knows to flow in channels,
    And how shores scintillate painted with their own natural pebbles,
And how sweetly the unsophisticated birds sing.

PROPERTIUS *Elegies I.2*

The seed is first stirred in us at the age

when maturity breathes strength into our joints... As soon as it emerges, issuing forth from its home, it is drawn out from the entirety of the body through all the limbs and organs, and comes together at certain points in the loins, instantly rousing the genital organs themselves. Stimulated, these parts swell with seed and there arises a desire to expel it towards whatever object the fierce desire strives for, and the body seeks out that which has wounded the mind with love.

LUCRETIUS
De Rerum Natura IV

33

Don't ask what will happen tomorrow.
Whatever the sum of days given to you,
Think of it as treasure,
And when you are young,
Never say no to dancing and sweet desire.
HORACE Odes I.9

NIGHT BANISHES SHAME,
WINE AND LOVE
TAKE CARE OF fear.

OVID
Amores I.6

Asklepias, in love with love,
Her eyes like a calm, blue sea,
Persuades everyone it's safe

TO SET SAIL FOR LOVE.
OVID
Ars Amatoria I

Dorian
plucked
a single
thread
of her
golden
hair,
Bound
my wrists,
and
took me
prisoner.

PAULOS
SILENTIARIUS
*The Greek
Anthology* V.230

34

IS AFTER THE MOON CLOVER

THE GREY WOLF

IS AFTER THE SHE-GOAT

THE SHE-GOAT

AND I'M JUST WILD ABOUT YOU.

THEOKRITOS
Idyll 10 (The Reapers)

Your
mouth
is a
hook
with
madness
in its
barb.

MACEDONIUS
*The Greek
Anthology* V.247

All women can be caught;
You'll catch them—

JUST PUT OUT THE NETS.
OVID
Ars Amatoria I

SOON
my flesh
AGAINST
your flesh
GREW RIPE,
OUR FACES
flushed
WITH HEAT,
AND OUR
sweet
whisperings
ROSE
AND THEN
fell away.

THEOKRITOS
Idyll 2 (The Spell)

AS THE SWEET-APPLE BLUSHES

ON THE END OF ITS BRANCH,

ON TOP OF THE TREE'S TOP-MOST FORK,

IT IS FORGOTTEN BY THE APPLE-PICKERS.

NO — IT'S NOT THAT THEY'VE FORGOTTEN IT,

THEY JUST COULDN'T QUITE REACH IT...   35

SAPPHO
fragment 105

It's a joy to walk
Where meadows are in bloom,
Where gentle Zephyros exhales his sweet breath,
To look on the vines of Bakchos,
And then to enter under the blanket of their leaves,
In your arms a silky girl,
Every inch of her redolent
Of the essences of Kypris.

THE ANAKREONTEA
poem 41

PARVA LEVES

It is an art to propel the swift ships with sail and oar;
It is an art to make the light chariot surge ahead;
And it is an art to pursue Love successfully...
She will not fall into your lap from thin air,
 that dream lover of yours.
She must be hunted down, in the first case,
WITH YOUR EYES.

OVID
Ars Amatoria I

*The secret keys to the shrine of Love
are in the hands of wise Persuasion.*

PINDAR
Pythian Ode 9

IF YOU SEE SOMEONE BEAUTIFUL, STRIKE WHILE THE IRON IS HOT.
YOU SHOULD SAY EXACTLY WHAT'S ON YOUR MIND.
GRAB WHAT YOU WANT, AND FILL BOTH HANDS.
FOR IF YOU START WITH "I RESPECT YOU,
I WILL BE LIKE A BROTHER TO YOU",
SELF-CONSCIOUSNESS WILL SLAM
THE DOOR TO YOUR DESIRES
IN YOUR FACE.

ADAIOS   *The Greek Anthology X.20*

CAPIUNT ANIMOS

If perchance a speck of dust happens to fall, as it sometimes does, on to her breast, you must flick it away with your finger: if there's no speck of dust, well then, flick off what's not there; don't leave any opportunity unexploited.

If her cloak is hanging down so it trails on the ground, have your eager hands lift it out of the dirt. You'll get a quick reward for your good work: the girl will put up with your eyes touching her legs thus revealed...

Small things fascinate little minds: it has proved useful to many to have a deft hand in the arranging of a cushion...

Be the first to snatch up the goblet that has touched her lips, and where she has sipped, sip there...

Make it your mission to ingratiate yourself with your lover's husband: once he's been made your friend, he will be all the more useful to you.

Tears, too, serve their purpose: with tears, you can melt the hardest steel. If possible, make sure that she sees your dripping cheeks. If the tears don't come (for they do not always arrive on order) then touch your eyes with a moistened hand.

OVID *Ars Amatoria I*

If you love,
Never unravel your genuflecting heart to its last thread,
Slithering in the oiliness of your own solicitations,
But practise safe seduction, subtly:
At least make a show of raising your eyebrows and
Looking at her in a faintly disparaging way.

AGATHIAS SCHOLASTICUS *The Greek Anthology V.216*

arte arte arte arte arte

The lover & ECHO

My dear Echo, please grant me a wish.
~ A WISH?
I want her to love me, but I don't think she can.
~ SHE CAN
Fortune's playing with me, I'll never have good luck!
~ GOOD LUCK!
Dear Echo, will you tell her whatever I say?
~ WHATEVER YOU SAY
See this coin – it's a pledge to give to her, please.
~ GIVE IT HERE, PLEASE
So Echo, will she ever be mine to win?
~ YOU'LL WIN!

GAURADAS
The Greek Anthology XVI. 152

I
WOULD
LOVE
TO
play
WITH
YOU;
YOU'VE
SUCH
a
GRACEFUL
way
WITH
YOU.

ANAKREON
fragment 402

Run along to the market,
Demetrios,
Pick up three
of those little grey fish
from Amyntas' stall,
And ten wrasse,
And two dozen
Plump prawns
– he'll count them for you.
Bring it all back here,
nd pick up six rose-garlands
From Thauborios...
Oh, and since you're passing,
You might as well pick up
My darling Tryphera too.

ASKLEPIADES
The Greek Anthology V.185

WHETHER THEY SAY
YES OR NO TO YOU,
all women love to be asked.

OVID
Ars Amatoria I

Let me be the one
To coil all round you,
Lead me astray,
And let your body
be the pasture
Where I graze.
And then, for all I care,
Let a stranger see me,
Or someone
From my home-town,
Or a traveller,
Lady-of-my-heart,
Or a priest,
Or even my wife.

XXXIX

39

PAULOS SILENTIARIUS
The Greek Anthology V.286

Galla, do say "No"; Love is glutted, cloyed
Without a long and winding path to joy.
Just don't say "No" too long, too often.

MARTIAL
Epigrams IV.38

GALLA

NEGA

THE SUM OF

CATULLUS, POEM 5. THE SAME MUCH-LOV

Come and let us live my Deare,
Let us love and never feare,
What the sowrest Fathers say:
Brightest Sol that dyes to day
Lives again as blith to morrow,
But if we darke sons of sorrow
Set; ô then, how long a Night
Shuts the Eyes of our short light!
Then let amorous kisses dwell
On our lips, begin and tell
A Thousand, and a Hundred, score
An hundred, and a Thousand more,
Till another Thousand smother
That, and that wipe of another:
Thus at last when we have numbered
Many a thousand, many a Hundred;
Wee'l confound the reckoning quite,
And lose our selves in wild delight:
While our joyes so multiply,
As shall mocke the envious eye.

RICHARD CRASHAW
(1613?–1649)
English poet

BOUNDLESS BLISSES

EM AS TRANSLATED THROUGH THE CENTURIES

YES! MY LESBIA! LET US PROVE
ALL THE SWEETS OF LIFE IN LOVE.
LET US LAUGH AT ENVIOUS SNEERS;
ENVY IS THE FAULT OF YEARS.
VAGUE REPORT LET US DESPISE;
SUNS MAY SET AND SUNS MAY RISE:
WE, WHEN SETS OUR TWINKLING LIGHT,
SLEEP A LONG-CONTINUED NIGHT.
MAKE WE THEN, THE MOST OF THIS —
LET US KISS, AND KISS, AND KISS.
WHILE WE THUS THE NIGHT EMPLOY,
ENVY CANNOT KNOW OUR JOY.
SO, MY LESBIA! LET US PROVE
ALL THE SWEETS OF LIFE IN LOVE.

WALTER SAVAGE LANDOR (1775–1864)
English writer

Lesbia, live to love and pleasure,

Careless what the grave may say:

When each moment is a treasure,

Why should lovers lose a day?

Setting suns shall rise in glory,

But when little life is o'er,

There's an end of all the story:

We shall sleep: and wake no more.

Give me, then, a thousand kisses,

Twice ten thousand more bestow,

Till the sum of boundless blisses

Neither we, no envy know.

JOHN LANGHORNE (1735–1779)
*English poet
(translation published
posthumously in 1790)*

LET US LIVE, MY LESBIA, AND LET US LOVE,
AND VALUE AT A SINGLE PENNY
ALL THE CARPINGS OF PERNICKETY OLD MEN.
SUNS CAN BE EXTINGUISHED AND REKINDLE:
FOR US, WHEN ONCE OUR LITTLE LIGHT IS EXTINGUISHED,
THERE IS JUST SLEEP FOR ONE UNENDING NIGHT.
GIVE ME A THOUSAND KISSES, AND THEN A HUNDRED,
THEN ANOTHER THOUSAND, AND THEN A SECOND HUNDRED,
THEN WHEN WE'VE CREATED MANY THOUSANDS
WE'LL STIR THEM UP TOGETHER,
SO THAT WE OURSELVES DON'T KNOW,
AND NOR CAN ANY GREEN-EYED MONSTER MAKE
THIS UNKNOWN QUANTITY OF KISSES
COUNT AGAINST US.

MICHELLE LOVRIC AND
NIKIFOROS DOXIADIS MARDAS,
1997

XLI
41

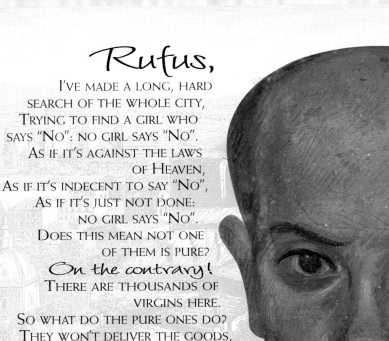

Rufus,

I'VE MADE A LONG, HARD
SEARCH OF THE WHOLE CITY,
TRYING TO FIND A GIRL WHO
SAYS "NO": NO GIRL SAYS "NO".
AS IF IT'S AGAINST THE LAWS
OF HEAVEN,
AS IF IT'S INDECENT TO SAY "NO",
AS IF IT'S JUST NOT DONE:
NO GIRL SAYS "NO".
DOES THIS MEAN NOT ONE
OF THEM IS PURE?
On the contrary!
THERE ARE THOUSANDS OF
VIRGINS HERE.
SO WHAT DO THE PURE ONES DO?
THEY WON'T DELIVER THE GOODS,
BUT THEY WON'T SAY "NO" EITHER.

SINCE FABULLA READ THAT
EPIGRAM OF MINE
IN WHICH I COMPLAINED THAT
NO GIRL SAYS "NO",
SHE'S IGNORED MY ADVANCES
ONCE, TWICE, THREE TIMES.
NOW, FABULLA, LISTEN TO ME:
I ONLY ASKED FOR A "NO",
NOT A *"No Way!"*

MARTIAL
Epigrams IV.71 and IV.81

42

HIGH SUMMER, HIGH NOON –

Languid limbs sprawled on the bed.

One shutter open, the other closed:
The semi-darkness of a forest,

Like flickering dusk
when the sun has just disappeared,
Or when night has gone
but it is not yet day,

The kind of light that's perfect for shy girls
Whose fearful modesty
hopes to find somewhere to hide.

Now look, Corinna's coming,
unloosened in her clothes.
Her parted hair shelters her pale neck...

I snatched at her dress –
not that it was much in the way –
Though she did put up a fight to keep covered.

43

But she fought as if she didn't really want to win.
She let herself down, my victory came easily.

So she stood before my eyes, perfectly naked
And utterly perfect.

What shoulders, what arms I saw and touched!
And what shapely breasts beseeching to be cupped!

What a smooth belly under a delicate waist
A side-view of immaculate proportions and dimensions,
And such a taut young thigh!

But why make a list? I didn't see anything I couldn't praise.
And I enclosed that naked body in my own.

Everyone knows what comes next. Spent, we slept together.
Please, O please, send me more afternoons like this.

SEND ME MORE AFTERNOONS LIKE THIS.

OVID
Amores I.5

YESTERDAY'S ROSE

With *her* repertoire of foreplay, she could have
revived an ancient oak, tempered steel and made a rock sing.

She was certainly up to arousing any living man,
But at that point I was neither alive nor the man I used to be.

What's the point in Sappho singing songs to deaf ears?
What use is it for a blind artist to paint?

Moreover, there was no end to the erotic fantasies I dreamt up;
No end to the positions I imagined or the variations I tried.

But the organ in question lay there, struck down before its tim
Disgraced, wilting worse than yesterday's rose.

OVID
Amores III. 7

HESTERNA LANGUIDIORA ROS

SENSUALITY

γλυκύπικρον
ἀμάχανον ὄρπετον

ONCE AGAIN,
Love the limb-loosener
sweeps me away.
Bitter-sweet monster —
there is no defence
against it.

SAPPHO
fragment 130

I'M GOING TO THE GARDEN
OF LOVE. MY BOSOM IS FILLED
WITH PERSEA FRUIT, MY HAIR
IS DRENCHED WITH BALM.

HARRIS PAPYRUS, 19TH DYNASTY,
NEW KINGDOM EGYPT.
Translated by Barbara Hughes Fowler, 1994.

*Iuventius, if I was allowed to
kiss those honey eyes of yours
As much as I'd like to,
I'd kiss them three hundred
thousand times,
And still not have my fill,
Not even if that kissing was
planted thicker
Than curved corn husks
in a field.*

CATULLUS
poem 48

XLV
45

EVEN TOO MUCH

O LEG,
O THIGHS
worth dying for
O BUTTOCKS,
O LITTLE OYSTER,
O FLANKS,
O SHOULDERS,
O SLENDER NECK,
O HANDS,
O BIG BABY-EYES
that I'm crazy for,
YOU'VE GOT
THE SNAPPIEST SYNCOPATION.
O UNMATCHABLE KISSES,
O SWEET NOTHINGS IN MY EARS,
Reducing me to rubble.

XLVI

PHILODEMOS
The Greek Anthology V.132

ὢ κατατεχνοτάτου κινήματο

IS NOT ENOUGH

EXTRAVAGANTLY,
they heat their blood
THE WHOLE WINTER LONG,
Oblivious to their kingdoms,
THE PRISONERS OF
flagrant desire.

VIRGIL
Aeneid IV (Dido and Aeneas)

WHOLE DAYS WITH HIM
she passes in delights,
AND WASTS IN LUXURY
long Winter Nights.
FORGETFUL OF HER FAME,
and Royal Trust,
DISSOLV'D IN EASE,
abandon'd to her Lust.

JOHN DRYDEN (1631—1700)
*English poet (translation from 1697
of the poem at left)*

47

NIGHT
AND
LOVE
AND
WINE
WANT
NO
HALF-
MEASURES.

OVID
Amores I.6

Either get out of here, or do it my way, woman.
I'm no old-fashioned gentleman,
I like my nights dragged out with dirty jokes and drinking:
You scurry off to bed in a mood after a single glass of water.
You like the dark: But what turns me on are
Love-games with a lamp as witness.
When I make my entrance, I want daylight on the matter!
Woolly underwear, thick tunics and camouflaging cloaks
Hide every inch of your body.
But from my point of view,
No female in my bed can ever be naked enough.
I'm the slave of girls who kiss like smooth-tongued doves:
From you I get the kind of peck
you give your grandmother at breakfast.
It doesn't occur to you to spice up the act
With wriggling, whispering and tickling:
You behave in bed like a priestess
Preparing the wine and incense for a funeral.

MARTIAL *Epigrams XI.104*

APHRODITE
MAY BE A
BITCH-GODDESS
IN ALL OTHER
RESPECTS,
BUT SHE
DOES HAVE
ONE VIRTUE
IN HER
REPERTOIRE:
A SWORN
VENDETTA
AGAINST
PRETENTIOUS
PRUDES.

AGATHIAS
SCHOLASTICUS
*The Greek
Anthology V.280*

Europa's kiss,

EVEN IF IT WENT ONLY AS FAR AS YOUR LIPS,
EVEN IF IT JUST BRUSHED THE CORNER OF YOUR MOUTH,
WOULD BE SWEET ENOUGH.
BUT EUROPA PILLAGES YOUR MOUTH
AND SUCKS YOUR SOUL
RIGHT OUT OF YOUR FINGERNAILS.

RUFINUS
The Greek Anthology V.14

You would find it simpler, my dear Lykinos, to count the waves of the sea and the flakes of snow falling from the sky than all my loves... One love affair has always followed another and before the last one is even finished, a new one begins... For fire cannot be put out by fire. My eyes are inhabited by some kind of mercurial gadfly with an insatiable and selfish appetite for anyone or anything beautiful — it's never satisfied, never at peace. I am regularly flummoxed as to why Aphrodite bears me such malice.

PSEUDO-LUCIAN
Erotes

PROPERTIUS
Elegies 1.19

XLVIII

HOWEVER LONG IT LASTS, LOVE NEVER LASTS LONG ENOUGH.

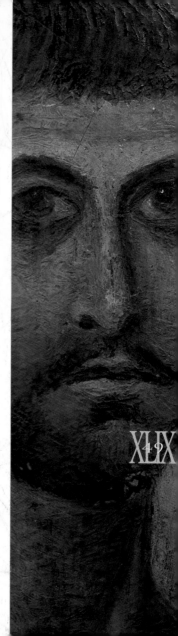

τò μεταξύ

*I don't want anything to come between us:
Even that thin fabric you wear
Feels to me like the Walls of Babylon.*

PAULOS SILENTIARIUS
The Greek Anthology V.252

WOULD THAT I WERE,
IF ONLY FOR A MONTH,
THE LAUNDERER OF
MY SISTER'S LINEN CLOTH!

I'D GATHER STRENGTH
FROM JUST THE GRASP OF
THE CLOTHES THAT TOUCH
MY BELOVED'S BODY.

FOR IT WOULD BE I
WHO'D WASH FROM HER SCARF
THE MORINGA OILS.
I'D RUB THEN MY BODY
WITH THE CLOTHES
SHE'D CAST OFF
AND SHE'D ...

WHAT BLISS I'D HAVE,
WHAT UTTER DELIGHT!
HOW VIGOROUS WOULD
MY BODY BE!

XLIX
49

*One of the love songs preserved on the fragments of a Cairo vase, from 19th or 20th Dynasty,
New Kingdom Egypt. Translated by Barbara Hughes Fowler, 1994.*

NOVEM CONTINUAS FUTUTIONES

Please my sweet Ipsitilla,
  My delicious morsel,
    My delectable treasure,
Order me for lunch today.
  Kindly see to it, if you will,
    That no one locks the door.
And don't you even think
  Of slipping outside,
    But stay home and prepare
For our nine-course non-stop orgy
  So, if I am on the menu
    Place your order straightaway:
For here I am, flat on my back,
  Already stuffed full of food
    But somehow still
      Poking up hungrily
        Through my tunic
And my cloak.

CATULLUS *poem 32*

DAPHNIS:
Even in an empty kiss there is sweet delight

AKROTIME:
I wash out my mouth and spit out your kiss

DAPHNIS:
You've licked your lips clean?
Then give them to me to kiss again.

THEOKRITOS *Idyll 27 (The Lovers' Talk)*

GOD SEND MY ENEMIES

MY DELICIOUS MORSEL

WHEN YOU HAVE FOUND
the places where a woman
loves to be touched,
Don't let shyness stop you
from touching them.
You will see her eyes
flickering with sparks of fire,
Just as the sun sometimes
gleams on clear water.
Next come the moans
and murmurs,
Sweet sighs and words
just right for the games of love.
But don't you race past her
with fuller sail,
Nor let her get ahead
of the course you've set,
But both should accelerate
to the winning-post
at the same time.
And the fulfilment
of desire is when
The man and woman
lie overcome together.

OVID
Ars Amatoria II

*Pleasure given as a duty
does not arouse me:
May no girl ever perform
a duty for me.
It gives me pleasure to hear
voices calling out in ecstasy,
Begging me to hold myself
back and prolong the act.
I like to see my lover
out of her mind...*

OVID
Ars Amatoria II

Either cross out

"GIVING LOVE"

altogether,

Eros,

Or add

"BEING LOVED", 51

So that you either

allay my

desire

Or alloy it

with another's.

POLEMON
The Greek Anthology V.68

OVID
Amores II.10

a celibate life!

DENIED ENTRY, THE WEEPING LOVER OFTEN
SMOTHERS THE THRESHOLD WITH FLOWERS AND GARLANDS
AND ANOINTS THE PROUD DOORPOSTS WITH OIL OF MARJORAM
AND, POOR FOOL, PRESSES HIS KISSES ON THE DOOR ITSELF

LUCRETIUS
De Rerum Natura IV

DREADFUL DOOR,

crueller by far than your mistress herself,
Why do you stand silent, outfacing me with such hard panels?
And why are you never unbolted to let in my love,
Insensible and unmoved by secret prayers you won't pass on?
Will I be granted no end to my pain?
Will I sleep ignominiously on the cold-blooded doorstep?
The waning night, the setting stars, the icy dawn and its raw breeze
All grieve for me lying here.
If only a word of mine could squeeze through an open crack
And seek out those lovely little ears and ring inside them!
... But you, you are the one, the greatest cause of my pain,
Dreadful door, never won over by my gifts.
The only one entirely devoid of pity for human suffering,
You answer me mutely with the silence of your hinges.

PROPERTIUS
Elegies I.16. From a classic of the "Paraklausthuron" genre,
the plaintive serenade at (and to) the mistress's barred door.

TO LOVE

ἐλέου δ᾽ οὐδ᾽   ὄναρ ἠντίασας

53

Konopion, I hope you one day sleep
The same way you force me to toss and turn on your cold doorstep.
Iniquitous woman, I hope you one day sleep
The same way you now send your lover to his rest.
You've felt no pity, not even in your dreams.
The neighbours are sorry for me,
But as for you — not even in your dreams!
But all these things will come back to you one day,
A sudden memory awoken by your own frosted hair.

KALLIMACHOS
The Greek Anthology V.23

COMING OUT WITH

OK, Cupid, I give in — I'm your new prisoner-of-war.
I'm coming out with my hands up.

OVID
Amores I.2

WATCH

ME

CLIMB

ONCE

LIV
54

MORE

THE

CLIFF

OF

LEUKAS

Whenever I lie on Kydilla's breast,
whether I come by day, or,
Audaciously in the evening,
I know that I am treading a precarious path
At the edge of a precipice.
I know that I am throwing all my dice
In the air each time.
But what good is knowing?
For you are high-handed, Eros,
And every time you drag me with you,
I don't feel even a phantom of fear.

PHILODEMOS
The Greek Anthology V.25

LOVE

CONVULSED

MY HEART

LIKE

THE WIND

SWARMING

IN THE

OAK TREES

AS IT

RUSHES

DOWN THE

MOUNTAIN

SAPPHO
fragment 47

And dive off into the grey waves,
Drunk with love.

ANAKREON *fragment 376*

ἐς πολιὸν κῦμα κολυμβῶ μεθύων ἔρωτι

MY HANDS UP

Sweet Mother,
I just cannot
sit at the loom
and weave today,
Soft Aphrodite
has enslaved me
with desire
for a boy.

Sappho
fragment 102

He
fell in love –
nothing to do
with apples,
rosebuds,
or curls –
just pure
madness.

THEOKRITOS
Idyll 11 (The Cyclops)

LV
55

**THE VOICE OF THE GOOSE SOUNDS FORTH
AS HE'S CAUGHT BY THE BAIT. YOUR LOVE
ENSNARES ME. I CAN'T LET IT GO.
I SHALL TAKE HOME MY NETS,
BUT WHAT SHALL I TELL MY MOTHER,
TO WHOM I RETURN EVERY DAY
LADEN WITH LOVELY BIRDS?
I SET NO TRAPS TODAY,
ENSNARED AS I WAS BY LOVE.**

HARRIS PAPYRUS, 19TH DYNASTY, NEW KINGDOM EGYPT.
Translated by Barbara Hughes Fowler, 1994.

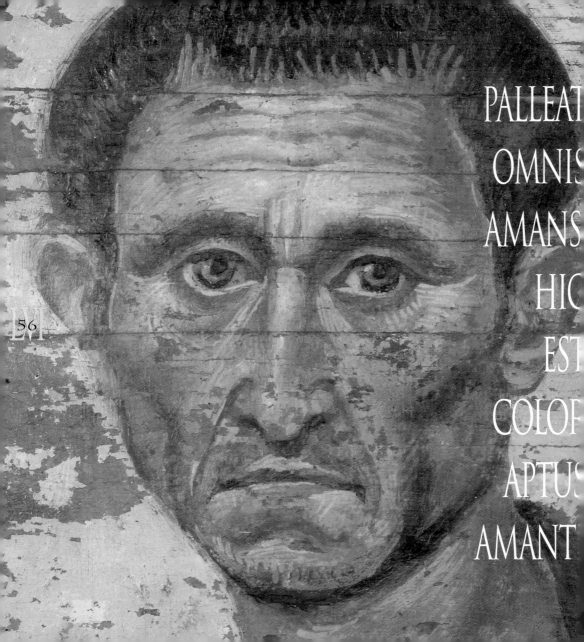

PALLEAT
OMNIS
AMANS
HIC
EST
COLOR
APTUS
AMANT

56

VERY

OVER

HOULD

E PALE:

HIS IS

OVE'S

PECIAL

HUE.

/ID
Amatoria I

In love,
Venus mocks lovers with images

AND THEY CANNOT EVEN GET SATISFACTION FROM GAZING DIRECTLY AT EACH OTHER'S BODIES, AND NOR ARE THEY ABLE TO SCRAPE ANYTHING OFF THE SOFT LIMBS WITH THEIR HANDS AS THEY WANDER HAPHAZARDLY OVER THE WHOLE BODY. AT LAST, WHEN WITH LIMBS ENTWINED THEY ENJOY THE FLOWER OF THEIR MATURITY, AND FINALLY THE BODY HAS A FORETASTE OF DELIGHT... THEY GREEDILY CRUSH THEMSELVES AGAINST THEIR LOVER'S BODY AND MIX THE SALIVA OF THEIR MOUTHS, DRAWING DEEP BREATHS AS THEY PRESS TEETH AGAINST LIPS. BUT IT IS ALL IN VAIN, SINCE THEY CANNOT SCRAPE ANYTHING OFF OR PENETRATE AND MERGE THEIR BODIES ENTIRELY INTO ONE ANOTHER. FOR THAT IS EXACTLY WHAT THEY SOMETIMES SEEM TO DESIRE, AND STRUGGLE TO ACHIEVE.

LUCRETIUS
De Rerum Natura IV

She has given half of herself to Desire, And half to Chastity. In the wasteland between the two, I loiter palely.

PAULOS SILENTIARIUS
The Greek Anthology V.272

sick for love

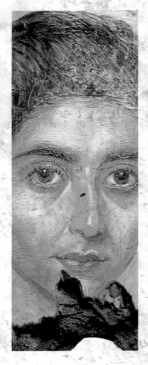

MELISSIAS SAYS SHE IS NOT IN LOVE,

But her body squeals as if it's been pricked

By a whole quiverful of arrows.

Her footsteps

And her breathing

Come in fits and starts.

Under her eyebrows – two sunken orbs

Shot down by darts.

I implore you, Desires,

in the name of your mother,

The beautifully-garlanded Kytherean,

58 Inflame the flesh of that repressed girl,

Till she confesses in a cry:

"Yes, I am on fire for him!"

Φλέγομαι

RUFINUS
The Greek Anthology V.87

MELISSIAS WILL NOT AVOW SHE SMARTS,

Tho' stuck all over with the tell-tale darts

Look how she hastes,

then stops love-struck,

in snatches

She draws her breath,

Look at Love's purple scratches

Beneath her eyes.

Scourge her,

deal Love,

till spurts

Of Blood,

or she will never cry

'IT HURTS.'

W.R. PATON
(translation from 1898 of the same poem left)

WHAT SHOULD I CALL IT, I ASK YOU, WHEN MY MATTRESS
SEEMS SO HARD AND MY BLANKET WON'T STAY ON THE BED?
WHAT AN ENDLESS NIGHT I'VE PASSED WITHOUT SLEEP,
THE TIRED BONES LAMENTING IN MY TOSSED-AND-TURNED BODY.
WOULDN'T I KNOW IF LOVE HAD TRIED TO HAVE HIS WAY WITH ME?
OR DOES HE CREEP UP CUNNINGLY, TO WREAK HIS HAVOC UNDER COVER?
THAT MUST BE IT. HIS SLENDER ARROWS HAVE PIERCED MY HEART
AND SAVAGE LOVE TOSSES AND TURNS IN MY VANQUISHED BREAST.
SHOULD I GIVE IN? OR BREATHE FLAME INTO THE FIRE BY RESISTING?

I'LL GIVE IN... OVID *Amores I.2*

OFTEN I'VE TRIED TO SINK
MY HEARTACHE IN WINE,
BUT PAIN TURNED
ALL THE WINE TO TEARS.
OFTEN I'VE HELD
ANOTHER GIRL IN MY ARMS,
BUT AT THE POINT OF ECSTASY
VENUS BROUGHT TO MY MIND
THE MISTRESS OF MY HEART,
AND DESERTED MY BODY.
THEN, LEAVING ME,
THE GIRL WOULD SAY
THAT I WAS BEWITCHED,
AND, HUMILIATED,
SHE WOULD TELL ME
THAT MY MISTRESS KNEW
THE ARTS OF HELL.
BUT MY MISTRESS USED
NO SPELLS TO POSSESS MY SOUL –
ONLY HER FACE,
  HER SOFT ARMS
    AND HER BLONDE CURLS

TIBULLUS
poem I.5

59

I will lie down within
  and feign to be ill, and then
my neighbours will come to see.
  She will enter with them.
She'll put the physicians to shame,
  for she will understand,
that I am sick for love.

HARRIS PAPYRUS, 19TH DYNASTY,
NEW KINGDOM EGYPT.
Translated by Barbara Hughes Fowler, 1994.

LACKING A

Fragment 31, a poem by Sappho, as translated through the centuries.

MY MUSE, WHAT AILS THIS ARDOUR?
MY EYS BE DYM, MY LYMNS SHAKE,
MY VOICE IS HOARSE,
MY THROTE SCORCHT,
MY TONG TO THIS ROOFE CLEAVES.
MY FANCY AMAZDE,
MY THOUGHTES DULL'D,
MY HEAD DOTH AKE, MY LIFE FAINTS,
MY SOWLE BEGINS TO TAKE LEAVE,
SO GREATE A PASSION ALL FEELE,
TO THINK A SOARE SO DEADLY
I SHOULD SO RASHLY RIPP UP.

SIR PHILIP SIDNEY (1554–1586)
English poet, politician and soldier

But when with kinder beams you shine,
And so appear much more divine,
My feeble sense and daz'd sight
No more support the glorious light,
And the fierce Torrent of Delight.
Oh! then I feel my Life decay,
My ravish'd Soul then flies away,
And Faintness does my Limbs surprize,
And Darkness swims before my Eyes,
Then my Tongue fails, and from my Brow
The liquid drops in silence flow,
Then wandr'ing Fires run through my Bloo
And Cold binds up the stupid Flood,
All pale, and breathless then I lye,
I sigh, I tremble, and I dye.

WILLIAM BOWLES
(translation from 1685)

FOR WHILE I GAZ'D, IN TRANSPORT TOST,
MY BREATH WAS GONE, MY VOICE WAS LOST:

MY BOSOM GLOW'D; THE SUBTLE FLAME
RAN QUICK THRO' ALL MY VITAL FRAME;
O'ER MY DIM EYES A DARKNESS HUNG;
MY EARS WITH HOLLOW MURMURS RUNG:

IN DEWY DAMPS MY LIMBS WERE CHILL'D;
MY BLOOD WITH GENTLE HORROURS THRILL'D;
MY FEEBLE PULSE FORGOT TO PLAY;
I FAINTED, SUNK, AND DY'D AWAY.

AMBROSE (NAMBY PAMBY) PHILIPS (1674–1749)
English poet

LITTLE OF DYING

τεθνάκην δ' ὀλίγω 'πιδεύης φαίνομ' ἔμ' αὔτα

AH! ... THOUGH 'TIS DEATH TO ME,
I CANNOT CHOOSE BUT LOOK ON THEE;
BUT, AT THE SIGHT, MY SENSES FLY,
I NEEDS MUST GAZE, BUT GAZING DIE;
WHILST TREMBLING WITH A THOUSAND FEARS,
PARCH'D TO THE THROAT, MY TONGUE ADHERES,
MY PULSE BEATS QUICK, MY BREATH HEAVES SHORT,
MY LIMBS DENY THEIR SLIGHT SUPPORT;
COLD DEWS MY PALLID FACE O'ERSPREAD,
WITH DEADLY LANGOUR DROOPS MY HEAD,
MY EARS WITH TINGLING ECHOES RING,
AND LIFE ITSELF IS ON THE WING;
MY EYES REFUSE THE CHEERING LIGHT,
THEIR ORBS ARE VEIL'D IN STARLESS NIGHT;
SUCH PANGS MY NATURE SINKS BENEATH,
AND FEELS A TEMPORARY DEATH.

GEORGE GORDON, LORD BYRON (1788–1824)
English poet (translation from 1806)

...At the mere sight of you
my voice falters, my tongue
is broken.
Straightway, a delicate fire runs in
my limbs; my eyes
are blinded and my ears
thunder.
Sweat pours out: a trembling hunts
me down. I grow paler
than dry grass and lack little
of dying.

WILLIAM CARLOS WILLIAMS (1883–1963)
American physician and writer
(translation from 1958)

LXI

61

...when I look at you, even for a moment,
I can no longer speak.
For my tongue has snapped in my mouth,
A sudden frail fire scuttles under my skin,
My eyes are empty,
My ears roar,
Sweat spills from me,
And trembling enmeshes me.
I am bloodless as grass,
And my life seems to hang
From a frayed thread.

MICHELLE LOVRIC AND NIKIFOROS DOXIADIS MARDAS, 1997

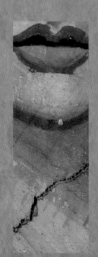

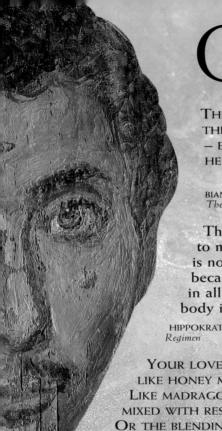

ONE SOUL IN

THIS NOBODY, THIS LOW-LIFE,
THIS ABJECT SLAVE
— EVEN HE IS LOVED;
HE IS MASTER OF
someone else's soul.

BIANOR
The Greek Anthology XI.364

The female and the male are able
to merge into each other, for each
is nourished by the other and also
because the soul has the same essence
in all living things, even though each
body is unique.

HIPPOKRATES
Regimen

YOUR LOVE IS MIXED IN MY LIMBS
LIKE HONEY MIXED WITH WATER,
LIKE MADRAGORAS
MIXED WITH RESIN GUM,
OR THE BLENDING OF FLOUR WITH SALT.

HARRIS PAPYRUS, 19TH DYNASTY, NEW KINGDOM EGYPT.
Translated by Barbara Hughes Fowler, 1994.

Ponticus, once a woman becomes yours,
She penetrates you ever more deeply,
Especially since you cannot tear
your empty eyes from her,
And Love, invisible until his touch
has bewitched your bones,
Forbids you to station yourself
at anyone else's door.

PROPERTIUS
Elegies I.9

SHE
WOULD
EVEN
HAVE
DRAWN
HER
SOUL
FROM
OUT
OF
HER
BREAST
AND
*surrendered
it to him...*

APOLLONIUS RHODIUS
Argonautica III

ACRIUS ILLA SUBIT
SI QUA TUAST

LXII

TWO BODIES

Kissing Agathon,
I found my soul on my lips;
For the poor thing came forward
As though it wanted
To cross over to him.

PLATO
The Greek Anthology V.78

"ADONIS, KISS ME, KISS ME FOR THE LAST
TIME,
KISS ME FOR FOR AS LONG AS A KISS CAN LIVE,
FOR AS LONG AS IT TAKES FOR THE BREATH
OF YOUR SOUL
TO FLOW OUT INTO MY MOUTH AND MY HEART.
I WILL INHALE YOUR SWEET LOVE-CHARM,
AND DRINK DOWN YOUR LOVE..."

τοσσουτον με
φιλησον, ὁσον
ζωει το φιλημα

BION
Poem 1 (Lament for Adonis)
From a speech of Aphrodite,
delivered as she kneels, overcome by
grief, over the corpse of Adonis, the
beautiful human youth she adored.
Adonis had been killed by a wild boar
and, according to the legend, the
red rose was born from his blood.

SHE'S ALWAYS THERE,

DEMANDING HER

POUND OF FLESH,

WITH HER HANDS

CUPPED.

TIBULLUS
poem II.4

It's only fair:
The girl who has just
plundered my soul
Should either
Fall in love with me herself,
Or give me a reason to fall
Irretrievably in love with her.

OVID
Amores I.3

LXIII

You alone, you alone are my home, Cynthia,
You alone are my parents,
You are my every moment of happiness.
Whether I come to my friends in sadness or in joy,
I will tell them: "Cynthia is the reason why."

PROPERTIUS
Elegies I.11

WE SHALL SHARE

A SINGLE SHORE FOR SLEEP,

A SINGLE TREE FOR SHELTER,

OFTEN WE WILL DRINK

FROM A SINGLE SPRING,

AND A SINGLE NARROW BED

WILL HOLD BOTH LOVERS.

PROPERTIUS
Elegies II.26

Look at Diokleia, just skin-and-bone,
*   a skinnier Aphrodite,*
But still cheerful in her own sweet way.
Now next to nothing will come between us;
I shall throw myself on her fragile breast,
And lie infinitesimally close to her soul.

MARCUS ARGENTARIUS
The Greek Anthology V.102

64

UNA UNA UNA UNA

It would be easier to tear apart
    two embracing vine-tendrils,
That have grown together
        twisted in an age-old plait,
Than to separate two lovers
    when they kiss,
Sinuous limbs knotted
    in an organic embrace.

PAULOS SILENTIARIUS
The Greek Anthology V.255

HE PROTECTIVE Arms of Love

My heart has a portion of yours.
　I do its will for you
when I am in your arms.
　My prayer is the paint of my eyes.
The sight of you makes bright
　my eyes...

HARRIS PAPYRUS, 19TH DYNASTY,
NEW KINGDOM EGYPT.
Translated by Barbara Hughes Fowler, 1994.

HE

WHO

KNOWS

HOW

TO

give

ALSO

KNOWS

HOW

TO

love.

65

YOU CAME,
　AND I WAS YEARNING FOR YOU;
YOU COOLED MY HEART,
　DRY WITH DESIRE.

SAPPHO
fragment 48

PROPERTIUS
Elegies II.26

ANYONE HELD IN THE ARMS OF LOVE MAY GO
　WHEREVER HE WANTS, SAFE AND SACROSANCT, WITHOUT FEAR OF AMBUSH.
　　THE NUMBING COLD OF WINTER NIGHTS CANNOT HURT ME,
　　　AND NO HARM WILL FIND ME IN THE MIDST OF A RAGING FLOOD.
　　　　I AM UNTOUCHED BY TROUBLE, AS LONG AS DELIA UNLOCKS THE DOORS
　　　　　AND ISSUES A WORDLESS INVITATION WITH A SNAP OF HER FINGERS.

TIBULLUS *poem I.2*

LESBIA'S

Catullus poem 3, as translated through the centuries

PITY!

mourn in plaintive tone
The lovely starling
dead and gone!
Pity mourns in plaintive tone
The lovely starling dead and gone
Weep, ye Loves! and Venus! weep
The lovely starling fallen asleep!
Venus sees with tearful eyes —
In her lap the starling lies!
While the loves all in a ring
Softly stroke the stiffened wing.

SAMUEL TAYLOR COLERIDGE (1772–1834)
English poet and critic

66

MOURN VENUS,

MANIFOLD IN WILES AND CHARMS!
MOURN, CUPIDS, VERSED IN ALL YOUR MOTHER'S ART!
MOURN, DAINTY CORPS OF GENTLEMEN AT ARMS,
SKILLED BOTH TO BREAK AND MEND A HEART!

AND WHY? HEARD'ST NOT, GODDESS, THE TIDINGS SORE?
THAT MY LESBIA'S OWN SPARROW IS DEAD!
HER SOUL! FOR WHOM SHE WOULD HAVE PLUCKED,
   SHE SWORE,
THE EYES OUT OF HER OWN FAIR HEAD!

HER DARLING, HER DELIGHT! HER HONEY-SWEET!
HE FONDLED HER AS BABE ITS MOTHER; HOW
EVER ROUND HER "PEEPED,"
   PULSED IN SHORT QUICK BEAT;
TREMULOUS FLUTTER TO AND FRO.

WILLIAM STEBBING, 1920

LUGETE, O VENERES CUPIDINESQUE

SPARROW

PASSER

WEEP, WEEP

ye Loves and Cupids all,
And ilka Man o' decent feelin':
My lassie's lost her wee, wee bird,
And that's a loss, ye'll ken, past healin'.

The lassie lo'ed him like her een:
The darling wee thing lo'ed the ither,
And knew and nestled to her breast,
As ony bairnie to her mither.

Her bosom was his dear, dear haunt —
So dear, he cared na lang to leave it;
He'd nae but gang his ain sma' jaunt,
And flutter piping back bereavit.

G.S. DAVIES
(translation from 1912)

MORTUUS EST MEAE PUELLAE, PASSER, DELICIAE MEAE PUELLAE

GRIEVE, GRIEVE,

Goddess of Love,
  Her Own Little Loves,
And, if there is any mortal out there
  Who truly loves Love,
    GRIEVE.
My lover's sparrow is dead,
My darling's darling sparrow
  is dead,
Whom she loved more
  than her own eyes.
He was honey in her hands,
  as intimate
With her as a girl
  with her own mother.
That sparrow seldom left her lap,
But danced on the air around her,
  here and there,
Forever making music
  for his mistress alone.

LXVII

67

MICHELLE LOVRIC AND NIKIFOROS DOXIADIS MARDAS, 1997

pleasure

I
HATE
LOVE

ALKAIOS
The Greek Anthology V.10

Desire
bites
you
with
its
sweet
tooth.

PSEUDO-LUCIAN
Erotes

FOR ME,
NEITHER THE
SWEETNESS
OF HONEY
NOR THE
STING
OF BEES.

SAPPHO
fragment 146

Delectable Diodoros,

Usually the one throwing his flames at young men,

Has been hunted down by the hungry eyes of Timarion.

He's skewered on the bitter-sweet arrow of Eros.

This is indeed a strange phenomenon:

Fire is in flames, roasting in fire.

MELEAGER
The Greek Anthology XII.109

& PAIN

ONCE EROS DIDN'T NOTICE A **bee**
SLEEPING IN AMONGST THE ROSES,
AND WAS STUNG.
STRICKEN IN HIS LITTLE FINGER
HE HOWLED TO THE HEAVENS
AND RAN A LITTLE, FLEW A LITTLE,
TO THE BEAUTIFUL KYTHEREAN,
CRYING "Mother, I am undone,
I am undone and I shall perish
at any moment.
It was a snake that savaged me,
A little tiny snake with wings,
The Beast the farmers call a Bee."
BUT THIS WAS HER ANSWER:
"If the sting of the Bee
Hurts you so grievously, Eros,
What kind of pain do you think is suffered
By those who are stung
With the arrows from your bow?"

THE ANAKREONTEA
poem 35

LXIX

If some god said to me
"Live, but without love",
I'D REFUSE:
my lover is so bad
— SO SWEETLY.

OVID
Amores II. 9

At the same time
Impossible and irresistible,
Silk and steel,
I can't live with you,
or without you.

MARTIAL
Epigrams XII. 46

τι λεπτὸν ψυχῆς ἔσω χάραγμα

A TEAR SIDLES DOWN MY CHEEK

A
TEAR
SIDLES
DOWN
MY
CHEEK,
A
SYMPTOM
OF
MY
INNER
LIQUIDATION
IN
SLOW
FIRES.

HORACE
Odes I.13

The Queen,
long since struck
by Love's savage tenderness,
Feeds the wound with her blood,
and is clutched by a
dark flame.

VIRGIL
Aeneid IV (Dido and Aeneas)

SPARE ME, I BEG YOU,
IN THE NAME OF THE
PACT OF OUR SECRET BED,
IN THE NAME OF THE LOVE
WE ONCE MADE,
IN THE NAME OF MY HEAD
BESIDE YOURS ON THE PILLOW.

TIBULLUS
poem I.5

Love

rejoices

not

a

little

in

being

showered

with

tears.

PROPERTIUS
Elegies I.12

71

Whenever I see lovers,
I recognize them straightaway:
They always have a fine imprint
Branded on their soul.

THE ANAKREONTEA *poem 27*

DEVASTATED

"I AM
SWEPT AWAY
BY THE FIRE
OF MY
FRENZY."

VIRGIL
Aeneid IV (Dido and Aeneas)

What use has it been
to fill the sky with promises,
NEAERA,
Wafting my many prayers
on alluring incense?

LYGDAMUS
poem III. 3

"DON'T LOOK AT HER,
or she'll ensnare you with desire.
For she captivates the eyes of men,
Devastates cities,
Burns homes to the ground.
This is her kind of sorcery.
I know her, and you know her,
And all who have suffered know her."

EURIPIDES
The Women of Troy.
From a speech of Hecuba, Queen of the fallen city of Troy,
warning against the deadly beauty of Helen, the cause of the
ten-year long Trojan war.

ὁρῶν δὲ τήνδε φεῦγε, μή σ᾽ ἕλῃ πόθῳ

BY DESIRE

BUT NEITHER THE TAWNY BOAR
AT THE HEIGHT OF HIS ANGER,
REPULSING THE MADDENED PACK OF HUNTING
HOUNDS WITH HIS LIGHTNING JAW,
NOR THE LIONESS SUCKLING HER UNWEANED CUBS,
NOR THE TINY VIPER TRODDEN BY A CARELESS FOOT
– NONE IS AS SAVAGE AS A WOMAN AFIRE
WITH THE DISCOVERY OF A RIVAL
IN HER LOVER'S BED.

OVID
Ars Amatoria II

Eros, stop aiming at my heart and liver:

If you really must shoot me,

Please try another organ.

MACEDONIUS
The Greek Anthology V.224
The liver was considered to be the seat of the passions,
and particularly of love and anger.

GET BACK INSIDE MY CHEST, HEART!

MELEAGER
The Greek Anthology XII.147

LXXIV

ODI

I HATE AND I LOVE. PERHAPS YOU'LL ASK WHY?
I DON'T KNOW. BUT I FEEL IT HAPPENING,
AND IT'S CRUCIFYING ME.

CATULLUS
poem 85

I HATE AND LOVE, WOULDST THOU THE REASON KNOW?
I KNOW NOT, BUT I BURN AND FEEL IT SO.

RICHARD LOVELACE (1618–1657)
English poet
(translation of the same poem, from 1659)

I LOVE AND HATE. AH! NEVER ASK WHY SO!
I HATE AND LOVE — AND THAT IS ALL I KNOW.
I SEE 'TIS FOLLY, BUT I FEEL 'TIS WOE.

WALTER SAVAGE LANDOR (1775–1864)
English writer
(translation also of the poem above, from 1842)

Love and hate are embroiled

Yet *again*, I love AND I DO NOT LOVE,
and I am mad AND I AM NOT MAD.

ANAKREON
fragment 428

μαίνομαι

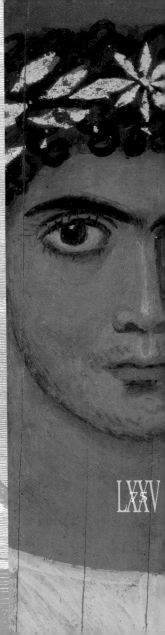

et amo

in a tug-of-war with my heart
(I think Love will win.)

OVID
Amores III.11

THE SEA IS AT PEACE, THE WINDS ARE AT PEACE,
BUT THE PAIN IN MY HEART IS NEVER AT PEACE.

THEOKRITOS
Idyll 2 (The Spell)

I have only half a life to breathe your beauty,
The rest is lost.
When you want me, I live like a God,
When you don't want me, *I live in darkness.*

THEOKRITOS
Idyll 29 (First Aeolic Love-Poem)

IF TO LOVE IS TO BE IN PAIN,
AND TO HATE IS TO BE IN PAIN,
OF THESE TWO TORMENTS,
I WOULD CHOOSE THE ONE
THAT AT LEAST HAS SOME
PLEASANT SIDE-EFFECTS

EUENOS
The Greek Anthology XII.172

LXXV

ου μαίνομαι

EVERY LOVER

LOVE
BEAT ME
SEVERELY
WITH A
HYACINTH
ROD,
ὑακινθίνη   AND
ῥάβδῳ   SPURRED
ME
TO RUN
WITH HIM.

THE ANAKREONTEA
poem 31

SO,
VENUS,
IT'S
WAR
AGAIN,
AFTER
A LONG
CEASE-FIRE.
PLEASE,
PLEASE
SPARE ME.

HORACE
Odes IV.1

I'VE PUT UP A WANTED POSTER FOR EROS THE WILD ONE,
FOR JUST NOW AT DAWN HE FLEW OUT OF HIS BED AND INTO THIN AIR.
γλυκύδακρυς   THAT BOY IS A SALT-SWEET TEAR, NEVER STOPS TALKING, HE'S A REAL TEARAWAY,
ἀείλαλος   CYNICAL, LAUGHING WITH A SNEER, WINGS AND A QUIVER ON HIS BACK.
I COULDN'T SAY WHO HIS FATHER WAS, FOR NEITHER HEAVEN NOR EARTH
ὠκύς   WILL ADMIT TO GIVING BIRTH TO THE LITTLE REPROBATE,
AND NOR WILL THE SEA, BECAUSE NO ONE, ANYWHERE, CAN BEAR HIM.
ἀθαμβής   BUT WATCH OUT, EVEN AS WE SPEAK HE MAY BE SPREADING MORE NETS FOR SOULS.
YES, LOOK, THERE HE IS LURKING BY HIS LAIR…
YOU HAVEN'T ESCAPED MY NOTICE, LITTLE ARCHER,
BY HIDING YOURSELF IN ZENOPHILIA'S EYES!

MELEAGER
The Greek Anthology V.177

FIGHTS A WAR

I was born
unfit for glory,
unfit for battle:
The only war
I'm destined for
is *Love*.

PROPERTIUS
Elegies I.6

"WHOEVER REBELS
AGAINST LOVE,
FACING OFF
AGAINST HIM
LIKE A BOXER,
HAS ALREADY
TAKEN LEAVE
OF HIS SENSES."

SOPHOKLES
The Women of Trachis

77

"*May you never appear to me as an enemy.*
May you never march on me beating a discordant drum of war.
For neither the sharp tongue of fire, nor the burning trail of the stars
Is more lethal than the dart of Aphrodite
Which speeds from your hands, Eros, son of Zeus."

EURIPIDES *Hippolytos*
From an ode sung by the chorus on the play's central theme, the deadly dangers of ignoring the powers of Aphrodite.

FETCH WATER, FETCH WINE, BOY, FETCH BLOSSOMING GARLANDS.
BRING THEM, SO THAT I CAN BEGIN
MY BOXING MATCH WITH LOVE.

ANAKREON
fragment 396

Punishing

"**LIAR!** Your mother was no goddess,
Nor can you follow your forefathers back to noble Dardanus.
You were spawned on the jagged rocks of Mount Caucasus,
And suckled by Hyrcanian tigresses."

VIRGIL
Aeneid IV (Dido and Aeneas)

LXXVIII

SPARKS ERUPTED
IN HER EYES,
AND SHE RAMPAGED
AS ONLY A WOMAN CAN —
A SIGHT AS TERRIFYING
AS THE SACKING OF A CITY.

PROPERTIUS
Elegies IV.8

EROS MUST
HAVE SHARPENED
HELIODORA'S FINGERNAIL,
FOR HER FIERCE LOVE-SCRATCHES
HAVE GONE ALL THE WAY
TO MY HEART.

MELEAGER
The Greek Anthology V.157

BITTER LOVE LIGHTS TWO FIRES
IN SULPICIA'S EYES.

THE GARLAND OF SULPICIA
poem III.8

I loved the lamplight brawl we had last night,
Especially the appalling abuse from your maddened tongue.

PROPERTIUS
Elegies III.8

Kisses

Lesbia hisses incessant curses at me,
And there's no silencing her spite
About me.
But if Lesbia isn't in love with me
Then I'm a dead man!
Where's my evidence?
Well, her symptoms
are the same as mine:
I curse her just as evilly,
But if I'm not in love with her
Then I really *am* a dead man.

CATULLUS
poem 92

Lesbia for ever on me rails,
To talk on me she never fails:
Yet, hang me, but for all her Art,
I find that I have gain'd her Heart:
My proof is thus: I plainly see
The Case is just the same with me:
I curse her ev'ry hour sincerely;
Yet, hang me, but I love her dearly.

JONATHAN SWIFT (1667–1745) *Irish-born English writer*
(another translation of the poem above)

For, indeed, at the very moment of possession, the passion of the lovers surges
and swells in irregular waves, not knowing what to enjoy first with eyes and
hands. They squeeze whatever meets their hands, causing pain to the body, and
they often force teeth into lips with punishing kisses. This is because the pleasure
is impure, and beneath it hide secret stings which incite harm to the very thing,
whatever it may be, from which the seeds of the madness spring.

LUCRETIUS
De Rerum Natura IV

JEALOUSY

WHATEVER HAPPENS TONIGHT,
TELL ME – CONVINCINGLY, PLEASE
– THAT YOU DIDN'T DO IT.

OVID
Amores I.4

If only you were beautiful
for my eyes only.

THE GARLAND OF SULPICIA
poem III.19

I LOVE EVERYTHING ABOUT YOU,
THE ONE THING I CAN'T STAND,
IS YOUR UNDISCRIMINATING EYE,
WHICH DOTES ON DISGUSTING MEN.

RUFINUS DOMESTICUS
The Greek Anthology V.284

Lydia, when you rave about
Telephus' rosy neck,
Or Telephus' soft white arms,
My god, my hissing liver swells
With swarming bile.

HORACE
Odes I.13
*The liver was considered to be the seat of the passions,
and particularly of love and anger.*

I SHALL SUFFER IF EVEN YOUR MOTHER GIVES YOU TOO MANY KISSES,
OR YOUR SISTER DOES, OR A GIRLFRIEND SLEEPS THE NIGHT WITH YOU.
EVERYTHING MAKES ME SUFFER, I'M SO NEUROTIC ABOUT YOU (FORGIVE ME!)
AND IN MY MISERY I SUSPECT THERE'S A MAN LURKING UNDER EVERY DRESS.

PROPERTIUS
Elegies II.6

Call yourselves friends?

READY TO DO ANYTHING FOR ME,

WHATEVER THE GODS THROW AT US?

WELL THEN, TAKE THIS MESSAGE TO MY LOVER,

JUST A FEW WORDS,

BUT NONE OF THEM VERY PRETTY.

LONG LIFE AND GOOD HEALTH TO HER

AND HER PARAMOURS,

THE ONES SHE SPREADS HERSELF ALL OVER,

ALL AT ONCE, ALL THREE HUNDRED OF THEM.

NOT REALLY IN LOVE WITH A SINGLE ONE OF THEM,

BUT AGAIN AND AGAIN, OVER AND OVER,

SQUEEZING EVERY LAST DROP OUT OF EVERY LAST ONE.

TELL HER NOT TO LOOK OVER HER SHOULDER

FOR THE LOVE I USED TO HAVE.

IT HAS BEEN DISMEMBERED BY HER,

LIKE A FLOWER AT THE EDGE OF THE MEADOW

SLIVERED BY THE PASSING PLOUGHSHARE

CATULLUS
poem 11

81

So, your husband will be coming to the same dinner-party as us?
I'm praying that it will be his last supper.
And I only get to gaze at you, as if I was just another guest,
While someone else has the pleasure of your touch?
You'll be there, nestling up to him, all warm and intimate?
Can he stroke the back of your neck whenever he feels like it?
No wonder that when they finally stopped drinking,
The centaurs went into battle over fair Hippodameia.
Now I may not live in a forest and I don't have a horse's rear end,
But it seems that I just can't keep my hands off you.

OVID
Amores I. 4. The wedding of Hippodameia to Peirithous, King of the Lapiths, was disrupted by drunken centaurs (mythical
creatures with the body and legs of a horse but the chest, arms and head of a man) who tried to carry off the bride and the other
women. The ensuing fight with the Lapiths is a favourite subject of ancient art, and is depicted on the metopes of the Parthenon.

INVIDIA

absence

When I remember your love,
  my heart within stands still.
When I see sweet cakes,
  they taste to me like salt.
Pomegranate wine was
  sweet once in my mouth.
Now it is the gall of birds.
  The scent of your nose
alone restores my heart.

HARRIS PAPYRUS, 19TH DYNASTY, NEW KINGDOM EG
Translated by Barbara Hughes Fowler, 1994.
The rubbing of noses and the smelling of the lover's face
were customary gestures of physical intimacy.

82

NOW SHE ECLIPSES ALL THE WOMEN OF LYDIA,
AS, AFTER SUNSET, THE ROSE-FINGERED MOON
  SURPASSES ALL THE STARS.
ITS LIGHT SPILLS OUT ON THE SALT-LADEN SEA,
AND ON THE FIELDS SWARMING WITH FLOWERS,
  WHERE BEAUTIFUL DEW IS DISTILLED
  AND EVERYTHING BLOOMS: THE ROSES,
    AND THE SOFT CHERVIL AND
    THE FLOWERING HONEY-CLOVER.
      BUT PACING TO AND FRO
    SHE REMEMBERS GENTLE AT THIS
    WITH DESIRE IN HER SOFT SOUL
  AND HER HEART IS DEVOURED BY PAIN.

SAPPHO
fragment 96

κῆρ δ' ἄσα βόρηται

& LONGING

YOUR FACE GAVE YOU AWAY IMMEDIATELY: YOU WERE IN LOVE
NOT JUST WITH LOST LOVES, BUT ALSO WITH THE MEMORY OF THEM.

PSEUDO-LUCIAN
Erotes

Poor
lovesick
soul,
don't
wrap
yourself
in the
mimed
warmth
of
dreams
filled
with
images
of
beauty.

MELEAGER
*The Greek
Anthology XII. 125*

83

There was neither ...
    nor shrine ...
from which we
    were absent,
no grove ... dance
    ... sound ...

SAPPHO
fragment 94

*So, there are ghosts amongst us after all.
Death is not the end of everything,
And the pale shade escapes the stifled embers of the funeral pyre.
For a vision of my Cynthia came to me, leaning over my bed —
My Cynthia, lately buried to the howl of a funeral trumpet —
In the heavy oblivion which followed the burial rites of my love,
as I bemoaned the cold kingdom of my bed.*

PROPERTIUS
Elegies IV. 7

ETUM NON OMNIA FINIT

Time Pours Past

If only I could come to you
As if I were a wingless Sleep,
Washing over your eyelids.

MELEAGER
The Greek Anthology V.171
The God of Sleep is traditionally depicted as winged.

FOR IF THE OBJECT OF Y

I grieve

"THAT MY MOTHER DID NOT BEAR ME FINNED LIKE A FISH,
THAT I MIGHT DIVE DOWN INTO THE OCEAN,
AND KISS YOUR HAND — IF NOT YOUR MOUTH.
AND I WOULD BRING YOU WHITE LILIES OR
THE RED PETALS OF VELVET POPPIES BURST OPEN.
BUT EVEN NOW, MY DARLING, I WILL LEARN TO SWIM …
SO I MAY TASTE OF THE SWEETNESS TO BE HAD,
LIVING WITH YOU IN THE DIM DEPTHS!"

THEOKRITOS
Idyll 11 (The Cyclops)
The Cyclops, Polyphemus, was in love with the sea-nymph Galatea,
and here laments their fundamental, and ultimately insurmountable, incompatibility.

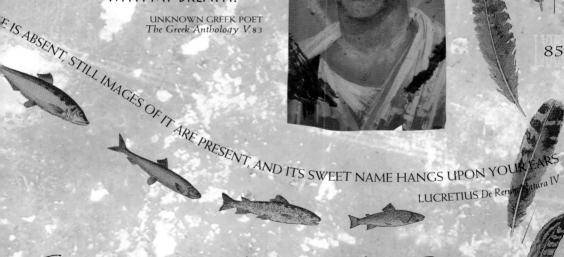

and I Lie Alone

I WOULD LIKE TO BE THE WIND,
SO THAT AS YOU WALKED
ALONG THE SEASHORE
YOU COULD BARE YOUR BREASTS
AND LET ME
CARESS YOU
WITH MY BREATH.

UNKNOWN GREEK POET
The Greek Anthology V. 83

85

E IS ABSENT, STILL IMAGES OF IT ARE PRESENT, AND ITS SWEET NAME HANGS UPON YOUR EARS

LUCRETIUS *De Rerum Natura IV*

The moon has set, and the stars of the Pleiades.
It is midnight; time pours past and I lie alone.

παρὰ δ' ἔρχετ' ὤρα

SAPPHO
fragment 168
The Pleiades was a constellation of seven stars named after the mythical daughters of the Titan Atlas.

RESTORATION

He was weeping, embracing his much-loved and faithful wife, just as when welcome land appears to the survivors, whose sturdy ship Poseidon has wrecked on the sea breaking it up with winds and mighty waves. Then a few have escaped the grey depths, and swim for land, their bodies saturated with brine, and, delirious with joy, they reach shore and escape these horrors. Just as welcome to her was the sight of her husband. And she would not, even for one single moment, loosen her white arms from around his neck.

HOMER
Odyssey
XXIII

LXXXVI
86

You have come,
dear heart,
you have come
At dawn after two days
and nights have passed
(Those who pine for love
become old men in just a day).
Just as Spring is sweeter than winter,
And apples sweeter than damsons,
And a mother-ewe shaggier
than her little lamb,
And a virgin more covetable
than a woman three-times married,
As the fawn is more delicate than the calf,
And the nightingale most crystal-voiced of all the birds,
So I am overjoyed at the sight of you,
And I run to you as the traveller runs
Towards shade when scorched by the sun.

THEOKRITOS
Idyll XII (The Beloved)

οἱ δὲ
ποθεῦντες
ἐν ἤματι
γηράσκουσιν

N AMBIGUO
VERBUM
ACULATA
ELIQUIT

From the heart of the fountain of delights arises something chokingly bitter in the midst of the very flowers ... either because she didn't explain some little word she tossed out, which now becomes welded to his needy heart and bursts into life in flames, or because he thinks she's been casting her glances around too freely, or gazing at another man, when he detects the trace of a smile on her face.

LUCRETIUS *De Rerum Natura IV*

There was a time, Lesbia, when you used to tell me That you were intimate with Catullus and only Catullus, and you wouldn't wish the King of the Gods in your arms rather than me. In those days I loved you, not just the way an ordinary man loves his lover, but as a father loves his children, and those who marry his children, who will carry his blood to the next generation. But now I've come to know you for what you are. I know you are cheaper, lighter by far, Yet I spend my love on you still more lavishly. How it is possible, you ask – In this kind of love, this kind of betrayal makes the lover love more, but like less.

CATULLUS *poem 72*

Is it me you are running from?
I beg you, in the name of these tears and of your right hand – since I've left myself nothing else in my misery – in the name of our marriage, in the name of our wedding night, if I ever did anything that was good in your eyes, or if anything of mine ever tasted sweet to you, I beg you to pity this house as its walls fall down, and if my prayers can still reach a place in your heart, abandon this plan of yours.

VIRGIL.
*Aeneid IV
(Dido and
Aeneas)*

LXXXVII

87

BETRAYAL

EFFICE PER MOTUM LUMINAQUE IPSA FIDEM

LXXXVIII

5619

TELL ME WHY YOU ARE SO NERVOUS,
PAINTING PERFUME ON YOUR BREAST
WHICH IS HOLLOWER THAN PAN'S PIPES?

ANAKREON
fragment 363

I know your promises are empty.
Your hair, still wet and breathing perfume,
Your eyelids still sagging from your sleepless night,
And the imprint left by a garland rammed on your head –
All these things betray your wantonness.

Your curls are uncoiled
By very recent ruffling,
And you lurch on loosened limbs,
Sodden on strong wine.
Leave me alone, woman.
Can't you hear the lascivious lyre and
Clattering castanets of the brothel, beckoning?

MELEAGER   *The Greek Anthology V.175*

IF YOU FAKE YOUR PLEASURE,
TAKE CARE HE DOESN'T SEE THROUGH YOU.
LEAD HIM ON WITH YOUR WRITHING
AND THE LOOK IN YOUR EYES.
DEMONSTRATE YOUR DELIGHT
WITH MOANS AND HEAVY BREATHING.

OVID
Ars Amatoria III

TEN MOUTHS,
AND AS MANY
TONGUES IN THEM
WOULD NOT BE ENOUGH
TO DESCRIBE ALL
THE HELLISH ARTS OF
WICKED WOMEN.

OVID
Ars Amatoria I

TIME CANNOT HIDE THE BASE METAL UNDER
THE FALSE GILDING OF YOUR COUNTERFEIT KISSES.

MELEAGER
The Greek Anthology V.187

You are so beautiful, I can't forbid you your indiscretions,
But you don't have to distress me with the sordid details.

I wish you had a little decency or at least impersonated the virtuous,
So I could believe that you are moral, even though you're not.

There is a place fit for naughtiness – fill it to overflowing
With every luscious indulgence, a million miles from modesty.

On your departure, let all your lewdness slip swiftly away,
And leave your sins behind in that bed.

That's where it's no disgrace to shed your clothes
Or for a thigh to be sealed to a thigh.

That's where your tongue can yield to bruised lips
And passion designs a thousand styles of perfect satisfaction.

That's where soft moaning and sweet nothings never stop,
And the bedstead shudders to the rhythms of love.

But before you go, put your blushing face back on with your dress,
And let demureness disown your dirty work.

OVID
Amores III.14

What a woman says to her desirous lover
Should be written on the wind and the running water

CATULLUS
poem 70

IN VENTO ET RAPIDA AQUA

PUDOR OBSCENUM DIFFITEATUR OPUS

LXXXIX

FIFTY WAYS
To leave your Lover

IT SEEMS TO ME THAT THERE'S NO MEDICINE FOR LOVE, NIKIAS,
NO OINTMENT AND NO BANDAGE — NOTHING BUT THE ARTS OF THE MUSES.

THEOKRITOS
Idyll 11 (The Cyclops)

If you love someone,
 and you wish you didn't,
Avoid contact
 to avoid contagion …

OVID
Remedia Amoris

90

Even mute places can hurt you.
Stay away from the places which once bore
 Silent witness to your love-making,
For they hold the seeds of sorrow:
 "This is where she was,
This is where she lay,
 This is the room we slept in,
Here she gave me nights of sensuous ecstasy."
 Brought back to mind,
Love is stung to life again,
 And the wound re-opens.

OVID
Remedia Amoris

There's no medicine for Love:

nothing you can drink for it,

nothing you can eat for it,

 no song you can sing

– there's nothing that works as well

as kissing, and caressing,

and lying together naked.

LONGUS
Daphnis and Chloe II

BEWARE OF RE-READING
 THE TREASURED LETTERS
 OF AN ALLURING WOMAN:
 RE-READING LETTERS CAN SOFTE
 EVEN THE STONIEST SOUL.
 CAST THEM ALL INTO THE IMPLACABLE FIR
EVEN IF YOU CAN'T BEAR TO DO IT,
 DECLARING
"THIS IS THE FUNERAL PYRE OF MY
PASSION."

OVID
Remedia Amoris

ON'T MENTION
ER SHORT-COMINGS,
CASE SHE TRIES
O GET RID OF THEM.

E WHO SAYS
ER AND OVER AGAIN
AM NOT IN LOVE"
IS IN LOVE.

OVID *Remedia Amoris*

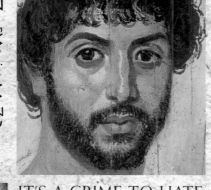

It is safer
to put out a fire
little by little,
than all at once.
Pull away slowly
and you will survive.

OVID
Remedia Amoris

IT'S A CRIME TO HATE
A GIRL YOU ONCE LOVED.
SUCH A FINALE
IS ONLY FIT FOR SAVAGES.
NOT TO CARE IS QUITE ENOUGH:
HE WHO ENDS LOVE WITH HATE
IS EITHER STILL IN LOVE
OR WILL NEVER LEAVE
HIS MISERY BEHIND.

OVID *Remedia Amoris*

XCI

A bad scar will open up
an old wound...
ou can't fight a fire next door,
So best keep out of the
whole neighbourhood,
d don't haunt the colonnades
where she walks
Or move in the same circles.

OVID
Remedia Amoris

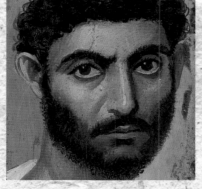

NEVER STYLE YOUR HAIR
JUST BECAUSE YOU
ARE GOING TO SEE HER,
AND DON'T RIPPLE YOUR
TOGA PROVOCATIVELY.
MAKE NO EFFORT
TO BE ATTRACTIVE
FOR YOUR ESTRANGED LOVER:
MAKE SURE SHE'S JUST
ONE OF THE CROWD.

OVID *Remedia Amoris*

I Wonder Who's Kissing Her Now?

O NIGHT, O MY UNSLEEPING DESIRE FOR HELIODORA…
IS THERE NOTHING LEFT OF HER LOVE FOR ME?
IS THERE NO WARMTH LEFT IN THE COLD IMAGE
OF MY REMEMBERED KISSES?
ARE TEARS HER ONLY BED-FELLOWS NOW?

MELEAGER
The Greek Anthology V. 166

92

Who's the slender boy,
soused with sweet scents, Pyrrha,
Who pushes you on to a bed of roses
in your welcoming grotto?
For whom do you
lash back your yellow hair
With that easy style?
Ah, how often he will be hurt to tears
By your wavering fidelity – and that of the Gods –
Staggered at this strange sea embittered by black winds.
He who enjoys you now, believing you are made of gold,
Hopes you will always be there for him, will always be his lover.
He doesn't know that the breeze deceives. Poor fools,
All those for whom you shine deliciously, when not yet tasted.
As for me, a stone in the temple wall shows where
I have hung up my dripping clothes,
An offering to the prevailing God of the Sea.

HORACE
Odes I.5

MISERI, QUIBUS INTEMPTATA NITE

REGRETS

THE DICE OF LOVE ARE MADNESS AND MAYHEM

ANAKREON *fragment 398*

AT DAWN, STILL IN HIS MOTHER'S LAP,
THE BABY EROS WAS PLAYING DICE
AND GAMBLED AWAY MY LIFE'S BREATH.

MELEAGER
The Greek Anthology XII.47

Poor damned Catullus, stop being idiotic,
　And recognize as loss the loss you can see.
Yesterday, the white-heat of the sun pulsed for you
　When you always went wherever she led you –
She, who was loved by you as no one else will ever be loved –
　When your desire was teased, many times, many ways,
And nor did she perform unwillingly.
　Yes, the white-heat of the sun pulsed for you.
But today she doesn't want you.
　And, stripped of your power, you must not want her either.
Don't keep chasing her escaping shadow,
　Don't live in desperation like the poor and the damned,
But be a survivor, be brave, don't melt.
　Goodbye, girl, from now on unmelting Catullus
Will not ask for you, will not look for what doesn't want him.
　But the day will come when you will be sorry,
When no one is there begging for you.
　Poor bitch, what dregs of life will be left for you?
Who will call on you then? In whose eyes will you be beautiful?
　Who will you love? Whose will they say you are?
Who will you kiss? Whose lips will you nibble?
　But stay steely, Catullus – don't melt now!

Catullus
poem 8

Winged Loves,
WHY IS IT THAT YOU'VE SUCH A TALENT
　　　FOR FLYING STRAIGHT AT US,
BUT YOU BECOME QUITE PATHETIC
　　　WHEN IT COMES TO FLYING AWAY?

MELEAGER
The Greek Anthology V.212

It's hard not to fall in love,

It's hard to fall in love, too,

　But hardest of all

Is to lose, having loved.

THE ANAKREONTEA
poem 29

LIGHT OF MY LIFE, MAY I NEVER EVER AGAIN
　　CAUSE YOU SUCH AGONY
AS I SEEM TO HAVE DONE A FEW DAYS AGO.
NEVER IN ALL MY FOOLISH DAYS OF YOUTH
　　DID I EVER DO ANYTHING
　THAT I CAN ADMIT TO REGRETTING MORE
THAN THAT I LEFT YOU ALONE THAT NIGHT,
WANTING TO PLAY DOWN MY DESIRE FOR YOU.

THE GARLAND OF SULPICIA
poem III.18

Let it always be like this,
    just like this,
        A never-ending festival,
Lying with you, mouth to mouth,
Nothing to do,
        nothing to be ashamed of.
In this there is, there has been,
    and there will be,
        For a long time to come,
Nothing but delight,
    Never diminishing,
        Always just beginning.

Attribution uncertain, preserved with the work of Petronius.

THOSE YEARS WHICH DESTINY

Yes, in the name of soft-haired Timo's curls
    Which love to be caressed,
Yes, in the name of Demo's skin
    Which robs sleep and breathes perfume,
And Yes again,
    In the name of Ilias' beloved love-games,
And of my night-owl lamp
    Which lit up all my many rites of passion,
I swear I have just a little breath left on my lips, Eros.
    But if you want that too, just say the word,
And I will tear it out of my throat for you.

MELEAGER
The Greek Anthology V. 197

UNDYING LOVE

No woman will be able to wrest me away
from the words I will weep at your door, my darling, my life.
I will always be stopping sailors and asking them
"Tell me, what port shelters my beloved?"
And then this is what I will say:
"Whether she lands on the furthest shores,
Or sails even beyond them,
She will always be mine."

PROPERTIUS
Elegies 1.8

*ILLA
FUTURA
MEAST*

HREADS OUT FOR ME
— Couldn't I spend them with you?

OVID
Amores 1.3

"Even when I'm gone,
I shall pursue you with dark fires,
And when cold death
tears my soul from my body,
Wherever you are,
my ghost will be there too."

VIRGIL
Aeneid IV (Dido and Aeneas)

MNIBUS UMBRA LOCIS ADERO

CYNTHIA

WAS

THE

FIRST,

CYNTHIA

WILL

BE

THE

LAST.

XCVI

96

PROPERTIUS
Elegies I.12

STIR STRONG WINE

INTO MY ASHES.

INTOXICATE

WHAT'S LEFT OF M[E]

BEFORE YOU PUT I[T]

UNDER THE EARTH

AND INSCRIBE THIS

ON MY URN:

"A GIFT TO DEATH

FROM LOVE."

MELEAGER
The Greek Anthology XII.74

ΔΩΡΟΝ ΕΡΩΣ ΑΙΔΗΙ

I
WILL
SIT
BOUND
BY
THE
ALTARS
OF
INVIOLABLE
VENUS.

THE GARLAND OF SULPICIA
poem III.19

SED
VENERIS
SANCTAE
CONSIDAM
VINCTUS
AD
ARAS